One Another Christianity

by Roger Hillis

ONESTONE

BIBLICAL RESOURCES

Published by:
One Stone Press
979 Lovers Lane
Bowling Green, KY 42103

Printed in the United States of America

ISBN 13: 978-1-941422-31-1

www.onestone.com

Contents

About the Author

About the author: Roger Hillis is a native of the state of Illinois. He received his education at Butler University in Indianapolis, Indiana, graduating from the College of Pharmacy in 1976. He has spent much of his life doing both pharmacy work and ministry work. He has worked with churches in the states of Illinois, Florida and Kentucky. He currently works with an independent retail pharmacy while also serving as evangelist and teacher with the Expressway church of Christ in Louisville, Kentucky. Roger and his wife Lisa have two wonderful children, Lesley and Jeremy.

You can reach Roger at his email: rlhillis@juno.com.

Dedication

To Lisa, Lesley, and Jeremy,

For all of the love and happiness you have
brought me throughout our lives together.

Foreword

The word church conveys to many Christians the idea of an institution. They often, I suspect, envision it as an entity apart from the members themselves. It is thought of as a corporation or organization that functions through leaders and a corporate head. Though the church is overseen by elders and served by deacons on the congregational level, it is essentially a body of disciples who function individually under the authority of Christ.

That means the church cannot function unless the Christians are active. Paul's favorite portrait of the church at work is a body with many members. "For the body is not one member, but many," he wrote (1 Corinthians 12:14). In another epistle he said that the church is "one body in Christ, and severally members one of another" (Romans 12:5). As a physical body can only function when all its members do their work, so it is in the church, the body of Christ. It can act only "according to the working in due measure of each several part" (Ephesians 4:16).

This theme threads its way through every chapter, every paragraph, and every line of *One Another Christianity*, the latest book by Roger Hillis. The work is based on the "one another" phrase that occurs some 58 times in the Greek New Testament. There believers are told to love, serve, accept, admonish, encourage, greet, honor, forgive one another, etc. These duties and many others are analyzed in their biblical setting to highlight the reciprocal and mutual responsibilities that followers of Christ have toward each other in the body of Christ.

Hillis, in his usual style, is both brief and practical. He neither belabors his points nor interminably discusses them to the exhaustion of his readers. He presents the biblical basis for the thought in each chapter, draws out the relationship of the idea to members toward one another, and lists practical applications that grow out of the point. Every chapter lists obligations that include something for every member—from the most talented to the "least among you."

This is not a book just to read. This is a book for study groups. It needs to be read, it needs to be discussed, it needs to be applied. It has, in this way, the value of challenging and activating every member and, thus, the body. Members together can analyze its practical suggestions and each one can find something he can do for the Lord. The book has the power to bring to life the dead or indifferent church by highlighting activities that, in many cases, even the untrained and new Christians can perform.

The author gets to the heart of who we are as people of God. This book is not merely a "to do" list that disciples perfunctorily and dutifully perform. Chapter after chapter challenges the very character of the reader. When he writes about "love," or "service," or "forgiveness," he is calling from scripture for heartfelt, spirit-filled devotion to the Lord and to one another. The book calls for change in the Lord's disciples, for in depth self-examination, for growth and development unto the measure of the fullness of Jesus.

This is the value of the "one another" study. It challenges each disciple but it affects the entire body. What each Christian does toward other Christians impacts both what he becomes in relation to God and what he develops with other followers in Christ. By affecting the entire church the book brings to fruition God's design for every member and the body as a whole.

If there is any complaint that preachers hear in every place, it is that members of the body, generally, are satisfied with mere attendance at every service. Few practice hospitality, take food to a new mother and her family, check on the widows to meet their needs, visit the hospitals, send cards to the shut-ins and others who are sick, greet and visit with one another at services, mow the yard of an indigent member, and on and on and on. When brethren are bonded together by the understanding and practices of these "one another" responsibilities, the body will go a long way toward active engagement in the work of faith and labor of love that God calls it to fulfill.

Our thanks to Roger Hillis for a book that is both practical and pertinent. It takes us back to the practices of the first-century church and to the essential character of that ancient body. It promotes a different kind of "restoration" among Christians—a restoration of the spirit of the church that Jesus built. It reminds us, as James says of the physical body (James 2:26), that the body of Christ apart from the spirit [of Christ] is dead.

I heartily recommend that Christians order this book, invite a few families into their homes, and in prayer and meditation, ingest and digest the theme and sub-themes of this important and useful work. This is not just a suggestion of a friend of the author and a reviewer of this book—I say this, brethren, with all seriousness. As an elder and evangelist in a local church, I plan to recommend this study for our teenage and adult classes.

When the contents of this book become the contents of our hearts, the body and every member will be as "living and active" as the word of God that indwells, empowers, and moves them (see Hebrews 4:12).

—L. A. Stauffer

CHAPTER 1

Members of One Another

"Just as each of us has one body with many members, and these
members do not all have the same function, so in Christ we who are
many form one body, and each member belongs to all the others."
(Romans 12:4-5)

The Bible uses many figures of speech to describe the Christian's
relationship to God, Christ and fellow disciples. We are:

- Branches in the vine – John 15:5

- Living stones in a spiritual house – 1 Peter 2:5

- Workers in a vineyard – Matthew 20:1-16

- Brothers and sisters in the family – Galatians 6:10

- Citizens in the kingdom – Ephesians 2:19

- Members of the body – 1 Corinthians 12:12-26

In 1 Peter 2:9, the apostle says of Christians that we are "a chosen people, a
royal priesthood, a holy nation, a people belonging to God." Each of these
terms or phrases illustrates or emphasizes some aspect of our relationship
with God and/or one another.

The Bible teaches the importance of being at peace with one another, be
devoted to, give preference to, be like-minded with, receive, encourage,

greet, care for, serve, bear one another's burdens, be kind to, forgive, submit to, bear with, teach, comfort, exhort, consider, confess to, have compassion for, be hospitable to, and above all things, have fervent love for one another.

As a matter of fact, the phrase "one another," taken from the Greek word, *allelon*, is found 58 times in the New Testament. Obviously, how we treat each other and interact together was of the utmost importance to God and the inspired New Testament writers. In too many places, the relationships between Christians are not strong and affirming as they were designed by God to be. I hope a discussion of these "one another" obligations to our brothers and sisters in the Lord will prove to be helpful, life-changing and perhaps, even eternity-changing.

Members of One Another

Let's begin our study by focusing on the statement that "each member belongs to all the others" or, as the New King James Version puts it, that we are "members of one another."

Paul reminded the saints (Romans 1:7) in first century Rome that they had mutual duties toward one another and the Lord which were fulfilled by using their God-given talents in His service. "Just as each of us has one body with many members, and these members do not all have the same function, so in Christ we who are many form one body, and each member belongs to all the others" (Romans 12:4-5). Using a familiar illustration of the human body, with many members, each possessing a particular and unique function, he encourages them to do what they can to serve God and to help one another in their pursuit of godliness. Rather than being a stumblingblock and source of discouragement to others, they were to keep in mind the influence that their lives and attitudes would have on others. He tells them, in verse 3, "For by the grace given me I say to every one of you: Do not think of yourself more highly than you ought, but rather think of yourself with sober judgment, in accordance with the measure of faith God has given you." He warns them against pride (the only disease known to man that makes everyone sick except the person who has it) and that God had gifted them to use their talents in His service, not in their own selfish pursuits.

Ephesians 4:25 says a similar thing, with the emphasis on honesty and integrity in our relationships. "Therefore each of you must put off falsehood and speak truthfully to his neighbor, for we are all members of one body." They were taught that truth, not falsehood, should characterize their dealings with one another. In context, he is teaching them of the distinction between the "old self," the corrupt, depraved man of sin and the "new self," a Christian "created to be like God in true righteousness and holiness" (verse 24). What they had become is vastly different with what they had been. As "fellow citizens with God's people and members of God's household," (Ephesians 2:19), they were to conduct themselves with purity and faithfulness. And as a reminder of what they now were, he emphasizes to them that they are "members of one another" (NKJV).

What does that mean? It means that they were mutual members of the same body and directly or indirectly connected to each other. It means that, in the kingdom, each has a different role to perform—based on ability and opportunity. It means, as Paul said it in Romans 14:7-8, that "...none of us lives to himself alone and none of us dies to himself alone. If we live, we live to the Lord; and if we die, we die to the Lord. So, whether, we live or die, we belong to the Lord." And because all Christians belong to the Lord, we share that in common and, therefore, are members of one another because "each member belongs to all the others."

The Body in 1 Corinthians 12

The classic passage in the Bible for a discussion of the various members of the body functioning together in the Lord's work is 1 Corinthians 12. The immediate subject was spiritual gifts, but the principles apply to every aspect of our work in the kingdom.

"The body is a unit, though it is made up of many parts; and though all its parts are many, they form one body. So it is with Christ. For we were all baptized by one Spirit into one body—whether Jews or Greeks, slave or free—and we were all given the one Spirit to drink. Now the body is not made up of one part but of many" (1 Corinthians 12:12-14). This passage shows us that we are all in the same body, but we are not all the same. We should not all be expected to do the same things as every one else. God doesn't expect that and we shouldn't either.

I saw a filler question in a church bulletin a few years ago that posed this challenge: "If everyone else were just like me, what would this church be like?" There are many applications we could make to that scenario.

If Everyone Were Like Me

If everyone else attended services just like I do, what would the attendance be? Would we have Sunday evening services or a mid-week Bible study or prayer meeting?

If everyone else gave like I do, what would the contribution be, not in the amount given, but in the amount of sacrifice shown by the offering?

If everyone else practiced hospitality just like me, how often would others be served and shown love?

If everyone else tried to help restore those who have left the church to the same degree as I do, how much effort would be expended on trying to bring them back to God?

If everyone else demonstrated the same willingness I show to teach Bible classes, what kind of teaching program would this church have?

If everyone else reached out with the gospel to the lost at the level I do, how many souls would be saved?

How much food would be taken to the sick? How often would the lonely be visited? How many prayers would be offered for those who ask?

Doesn't that make you think? I hope so. We all need to evaluate our effort in serving in the Lord's work where we are members. But as valid as this kind of self-examination is, it overlooks an important reality. We are not all alike and we are not supposed to be. All members do not have the same function. We all have been given talents and opportunities by God and are expected to do what we can with them.

The fact that God has created us all different means that everyone, therefore, is both unique and important. We all matter to God.

"If the foot should say, 'Because I am not a hand, I do not belong to the body,' it would not for that reason cease to be part of the body. And if the ear should say, 'Because I am not an eye, I do not belong to the body,' it would not for that reason cease to be part of the body. If the whole body were an eye, where would the sense of hearing be? If the whole body were an ear, where would be sense of smell be?" (1 Corinthians 12:15-17).

We cannot use the excuse that, due to limited talent, we are insignificant. God does not allow members of the church to have an inferiority complex that paralyzes them from doing their duty. The one talent man in the parable (Matthew 25) was expected to use his money wisely and when he did not, he was punished by the master.

You have various abilities because that's the way God made you. "But in fact God has arranged the parts in the body, every one of them, just as he wanted them to be" (verse 18). Some people have been given much; others have been given less. But the Lord expects all of us to do what we can with what we have been given.

Also, we cannot exclude others because they are different from us. A superiority complex is just as sinful to God as a feeling of insignificance. Those who are greatly talented must use their abilities in His service and we should all be grateful for those five, ten and even more talented people in the kingdom. But we are not to elevate them above others and they certainly shouldn't think of themselves more highly than they ought. "The eye cannot say to the hand, 'I don't need you!' And the head cannot say to the feet, 'I don't need you!' On the contrary, those parts of the body that seem to be weaker are indispensable" (verses 21-22). We must not look down on others and elevate ourselves. I well remember some of the Bible class teachers in my youth reminding us regularly that the ground is all level at the foot of the cross. One repeatedly said, "There are no big I's and little you's in the church."

I repeat—everyone is unique and everyone is important.

Another Illustration

A local church is supposed to work together like an athletic team. Paul wrote in Philippians 1:27, "Whatever happens, conduct yourselves in a manner worthy of the gospel of Christ. Then, whether I come and see you or only hear about you in my absence, I will know that you stand firm in one spirit, contending as one man for the faith of the gospel." The phrase "contending as one man" is an athletic term that refers to a spirit of cooperation, love, mutual respect and devotion. The New King James Version renders that phrase as "striving together." It points out that the relationship between two Christians is to be a friendship, or as the Bible describes it, a fellowship, sharing together in good times and bad.

Someone has said that coming together is a beginning, keeping together is progress, but working together is success. And that is the spirit of teamwork that we need to have in the local church. Another writer describes it with the acrostic for **TEAM**—Together Each Achieves More.

"I appeal to you, brothers, in the name of our Lord Jesus Christ, that all of you agree with one another so that there may be no divisions among you and that you may be perfectly united in mind and thought" (1 Corinthians 1:10). That's what the Bible calls unity or, put another way, "members who belong to all the others."

Some Applications

As members who belong to one another, we have certain obligations to each other. Let me make three important observations.

1. All Christians must obey the "one another" commands. These are not responsibilities for only a select few, for those in leadership, or for those who have college degrees. It is not only for the spiritually weak who need some extra help to live faithfully. Every individual Christian has an obligation to meet the needs of other disciples, as outlined in these "one another" duties.

   "Do nothing out of selfish ambition or vain conceit, but in humility consider others better than yourselves. Each of you should look not only to your own interests, but also to the interests of others" (Philippians 2:3-4). Notice that the apostle puts the emphasis on "each of you."

"We ought always to thank God for you, brothers, and rightly so, because your faith is growing more and more, and the love every one of you has for each other is increasing" (2 Thessalonians 1:3). No one is left out of "every one of you." This is a universal responsibility. The specifics may vary from situation to situation and person to person, but the principle remains constant. We all must serve one another in the kingdom.

2. All Christians must obey all of these responsibilities. Paul said to the early Christians in Corinth, "The reason I wrote you was to see if you would stand the test and be obedient in everything" (2 Corinthians 2:9). The writers of the New Testament never envisioned the kind of discipleship in which Christians would choose which commands they would obey and which ones they would ignore. They were expected to be obedient to every duty and responsibility commanded by the Holy Spirit.

"Remind the people to be subject to rulers and authorities, to be obedient, to be ready to do whatever is good" (Titus 3:1). The New King James Version says, "to be ready for every good work." Whatever God tells us to do in our relationships with one another, we must do, if we would please him. We cannot disobey any of God's commands and please him (James 2:10-11).

3. We must obey them in relationship to all other Christians. We are limited, of course, by time, space, talent and opportunity. But to the best of our ability, we must do whatever we can for whomever we can, whenever and wherever we can.

These responsibilities are not to be fulfilled just with our best friends, our family, or those who are most likeable. And this seems to be a major part of the problem with many churches. They develop groups, often called cliques, and have those who are "in" and those who are "out." No such distinctions ought to exist.

"My brothers, as believers in our glorious Lord Jesus Christ, don't show favoritism. Suppose a man comes into your meeting wearing a gold ring and fine clothes, and a poor man in shabby clothes also comes in. If you show special attention to the man wearing fine clothes and say, 'Here's a good seat for you,' but say to the poor man, 'You stand there' or 'Sit on the floor by my feet,' have you not discriminated among yourselves and become judges with evil thoughts? ... If you really keep the royal law found in Scripture, 'Love your neighbor as yourself,' you are doing right. But if you show favoritism, you sin and are convicted by the law as lawbreakers" (James 2:1-4, 8-9). No "partiality" (NKJV) or "respect of persons" (KJV) is allowed. There are to be no differences in how we treat others, whether they are educated or uneducated, rich or poor, black or white, male or female. As Paul stated in Galatians 3:28, we "are all one in Christ Jesus."

A Place to Belong

We all need help from time to time and are supposed to be there for each other. The church is supposed to be a place where we can get help and find understanding, not criticism and suspicion.

The church grows and is strengthened as each individual member does his or her part. Paul says, "...speaking the truth in love, we will in all things grow up into him who is the Head, that is, Christ. From him the whole body, joined and held together by every supporting ligament, grows and builds itself up in love, as each part does its work" (Ephesians 4:15-16). That's one of the primary reasons God designed the church, so that we can all get the help we need from him, through the encouragement of our brothers and sisters in the Lord.

And this is not the kind of thing in which we can say, let someone else do it. It is my job. It is your job. It is our duty as disciples of our Master, as members of the church for which he shed his blood.

The kind of church we are talking about is a place to belong. We are going to talk about helping everyone become a real part of the group, making every member an active, working, growing member, having no divisions in the body, caring for one another, bearing each other's burdens, having fun together, enjoying each other's company, being best friends, meeting everyone's needs—spiritual, moral, financial, emotional—breaking down any barriers that exist, and being accountable to each other.

People need a place to belong, to feel loved and to be a vital member of the family. The church is to be a shelter from the storms of life. I want to go to heaven and I need your help. That's what this book is going to explore. Thanks for caring enough to read it and study this vital topic.

One Another Christianity

CHAPTER 2

Serve One Another

"For you, brethren, have been called to liberty; only do not use liberty
as an opportunity for the flesh, but through love serve one another."
(Galatians 5:13, NKJV)

In Mark 10:35-45, we read an interesting exchange between Jesus, James
and John (along with their mother, according to Matthew 20). It goes
like this:

> "Then James and John, the sons of Zebedee, came to him.
> 'Teacher,' they said, 'we want you to do for us whatever we ask.'
> 'What do you want me to do for you?' he asked. They replied,
> 'Let one of us sit at your right and the other at your left in your
> glory.' 'You don't know what you are asking,' Jesus said. 'Can
> you drink the cup I drink or be baptized with the baptism I am
> baptized with?' 'We can,' they answered. Jesus said to them, 'You
> will drink the cup I drink and be baptized with the baptism I am
> baptized with, but to sit at my right or left is not for me to grant.
> These places belong to those for whom they have been prepared.'
> When the ten heard about this, they became indignant with
> James and John. Jesus called them together and said, 'You know
> that those who are regarded as rulers of the Gentiles lord it over
> them, and their high officials exercise authority over them. Not
> so with you. Instead, whoever wants to become great among

you must be your servant, and whoever wants to be first must be slave of all. For even the Son of Man did not come to be served, but to serve, and to give his life as a ransom for many.'"

Everything about the life of Jesus was aimed at serving others. As he said himself, "For even the Son of Man did not come to be served, but to serve, and to give his life as a ransom for many." He healed the sick. He cast out demons from the tormented. He spent time with the outcast and downtrodden. His message was one of hope and encouragement. He gave light to those in darkness. Ultimately, he died on the cross as the ransom (the purchase price to free a slave) for the sins of the world.

One of the clearest examples of service in the life of Christ is found in John 13:1-17. This is the occasion when Jesus washed the feet of the disciples. "Jesus knew that the Father had put all things under his power, and that he had come from God and was returning to God; so he got up from the meal, took off his outer clothing, and wrapped a towel around his waist. After that, he poured water into a basin and began to wash his disciples' feet, drying them with the towel that was wrapped around him" (verses 3-5).

Peter didn't understand. "He came to Simon Peter, who said to him, 'Lord, are you going to wash my feet?' Jesus replied, 'You do not realize now what I am doing, but later you will understand.' 'No,' said Peter, 'you shall never wash my feet.' Jesus answered, 'Unless I wash you, you have no part with me.'" (verses 6-8). Simon Peter saw incongruity and contradiction in what Jesus was doing. And many still do not understand today. The concepts of "God" and "servant" don't go together in our thinking. We think of God as power, glory, purity and majesty and, of course, all of that is true. But our Savior was a serving Lord. It was his very nature. He did not become a servant in the incarnation. It was his heart (mind, attitude) of service that led to the incarnation in the first place.

The disciples' true intentions were exposed when Jesus found them arguing about who was greatest. Jesus told them that it was the one who could humble himself like a small child (see Matthew 18:4). Jesus was not teaching them how to wash dirty feet—they knew how to do that. He was teaching them to be humble and, in that humility, to serve others.

I need to point out that Jesus was not binding the religious practice of footwashing for his people for all time. There are several things in the context that lead me to that conclusion. First, in verse 7, when Jesus said to Peter, "You do not realize now what I am doing, but later you will understand," are we to believe that Peter didn't know Jesus was going to wash his feet? Of course, he understood that. But, it was the deeper meaning behind the action that Peter didn't understand. The same thing is true of the question Christ asked the whole group in verse 12, "Do you understand what I have done for you?" They were not always the sharpest bunch of students, but they did know what he had done. They just needed to be taught why he had done it and what they were to learn from the experience.

Also, the Master said, in verse 15, "I have set you an example that you should do as I have done for you." Notice that he did not say, do *what* I have done for you, but do *as* I have done for you. If their Teacher and Lord could wash their dirty feet because that was what they needed at the time, then no job should be too lowly for them to do for each other. If that was not beneath him, it should not be beneath them, either. And if that's what someone needs, we should be willing to do it. But he was not binding a specific method or practice on them; he was teaching them that, in humility and love, they should serve each other. It was the principle, not the specific, he wanted them to learn.

The Nature of a Servant

Serving others was not just an obligatory deed Jesus did. It was who he was. Everything about him was devoted to serving others and he wanted his disciples to have that same spirit.

But being a servant to others is not always easy. Our selfish nature seems to be more designed toward being served than serving. It is much easier to have people wait on us and do things for us. There is a certain streak of laziness in most of us. We need a change of heart. The Lord's work depends on those who work and serve, not on those who sit around and do nothing. When all is said and done, more is said than is done.

The contrast in Mark 10:35-45 is between the way the world thinks and how we conduct our lives in the Lord's kingdom. In the kingdom of the world, people achieve greatness by dominating others. Our society preaches, "If it feels good, do it." "Look out for number one." "Win through intimidation." Without thinking of others, the world's elite step on as many as necessary to make it to the top.

That can even happen in religious circles. The scribes and Pharisees of Jesus' day had a problem with that. Jesus reserved his harshest rebukes for the self-righteous. "Everything they do is done for men to see: They make their phylacteries wide and the tassels on their garments long; they love the place of honor at banquets and the most important seats in the synagogues; they love to be greeted in the marketplaces and to have men call them 'Rabbi.' But you are not to be called 'Rabbi,' for you have only one Master and you are all brothers. And do not call anyone on earth 'father,' for you have one Father, and he is in heaven. Nor are you to be called, 'teacher,' for you have one Teacher, the Christ. The greatest among you will be your servant. For whoever exalts himself will be humbled, and whoever humbles himself will be exalted" (Matthew 23:5-12). This was the major problem of Diotrephes (3 John 9-11). He wanted to be the master and have everyone else bow down to his wishes.

Jesus made it clear that, for those who would be his disciples, "Not so with you."

Characteristics of a Servant

There are three key characteristics of a servant. We need to learn and live out these lessons well.

1. Put others' needs first. The key question should not be "What's in it for me?," but "What do they need?" "Do nothing out of selfish ambition or vain conceit, but in humility consider others better than yourselves. Each of you should look not only to your own interests, but also to the interests of others" (Philippians 2:3-4). Too many people today focus only on themselves. The Lord says—think about the other person.

   Christ told an interesting story in Luke 17:7-10. "Suppose one of you had a servant plowing or looking after the sheep. Would he say to the servant when he comes in from the field, 'Come along now and sit down to eat?' Would he not rather say, 'Prepare my supper, get yourself ready and wait on me while I eat and drink; after that you may eat and drink'? Would he thank the servant because he did what he was told to do? So you also, when you have done everything you were told to do, should say, 'We are unworthy servants; we have only done our duty.'" In some ways, that seems unfair, doesn't it? Maybe it is, but that's life. The fact is that this parable defines servanthood for us. It shows us we must always meet the needs of others first, just as a servant obeys his master.

All of this is not very popular in a culture that is characterized by selfishness. People are far too focused on self and whatever they can do for themselves that they think will bring them happiness. It doesn't matter if it's money, sex, position or status. We are busy and competitive and woe to anyone who gets in our way.

To be servants of the Lord we must serve one another. Someone said it this way: "Service is love made visible." That's what it really means to serve others—see what they need and then do what you must to meet those needs. This is how James says we can demonstrate the genuineness of our faith. "Suppose a brother or sister is without clothes and daily food. If one of you says to him, 'Go, I wish you well; keep warm and well fed,' but does nothing about his physical needs; what good is it? In the same way, faith by itself, if it is not accompanied by action, is dead" (James 2:15-17).

2. Prepare to be inconvenienced. Opportunities to serve others are often overlooked and left undone because they are usually not convenient. Helping others takes time and effort (see Luke 10:30-35). The priest and the Levite were simply not willing to get involved. The one you would least expect (at least, the last one a Jew would expect), the Samaritan, did what it took to meet the needs of the wounded sojourner. Do you suppose the Samaritan could really spare the time? Or the effort? Or the money?

Jesus left the glories of heaven to come to the earth as a man and then to die on the cross for the sins of a mostly ungrateful world. How inconvenient that must have been! But that is the context of Paul's comments to the Philippians about service. "Your attitude should be the same as that of Christ Jesus: Who, being in very nature God, did not consider equality with God something to be grasped, but made himself nothing, taking the very nature of a servant, being made in human likeness. And being found in appearance as a man, he humbled himself and became obedient to death—even death on a cross!" (Philippians 2:5-8). We must never forget that he didn't have to do that. He did it because he loved us and wanted to serve our needs. And so, he did what only he could do. He lived a perfect life and died the perfect death. I repeat—how inconvenient! That's the way it is with service.

It takes time to visit the sick, study the Bible with someone, and be a friend to the lonely and distressed. Anything that is truly worthwhile usually does. But it is worth it and that is just a part of what service really is.

John Wesley is reported to have said:

> "Do all the good you can, by all the means you can,
>
> In all the ways you can, in all the places you can,
>
> At all the times you can, to all the people you can,
>
> As long as ever you can."

I wish I'd said that. I wish I lived it out better than I do.

3. Serve in unnoticed ways. "Be careful not to do your 'acts of righteousness' before men, to be seen by them. If you do, you will have no reward from your Father in heaven. So when you give to the needy, do not announce it with trumpets, as the hypocrites do in the synagogues and on the streets, to be honored by men. I tell you the truth, they have received their reward in full. But when you give to the needy, do not let your left hand know what your right hand is doing, so that your giving may be in secret. Then your Father, who sees what is done in secret, will reward you" (Matthew 6:1-4). We must be involved in the day to day

lives of others—helping, encouraging, praying, working, serving even if no one else ever knows about it.

There are many people who love God and others who don't receive much praise: Bible class teachers, moms who cook the meals and wash the dirty clothes, those who unlock and lock the church building, prepare the communion, clean the building, mow the grass, people who invite their neighbors to study the Bible or who are trying to set a good example at work to influence others for God. These people don't do these things to be praised by others and would be embarrassed to have their names brought up in a public way. These people are only concerned about meeting the needs of others, no matter who gets the credit. Their goal is to glorify God in all they do. As the Savior said it, "In the same way, let your light shine before men, that they may see your good deeds and praise your Father in heaven" (Matthew 5:16). To God be the glory for each and every faithful disciple.

Don't get me wrong. We all appreciate a pat on the back or a sincere word of thanks or a kind note (or maybe just a smile when we need it most). But that's not why we serve. That's just one of the benefits. We serve to obey our Lord.

Some Practical Suggestions

Many Christians do not understand what is really involved in being a servant. Perhaps a few examples will serve to illustrate. Serving is:

- Buying groceries for a needy family.

- Inviting some less fortunate people to your home for a evening of food and fellowship.

- Serving in a homeless shelter in your city.

- Buying clothing or a pair of shoes for someone who cannot afford them.

- Paying for medicine for a sick child or adult.

- Giving someone who cannot drive or who doesn't have a car a ride to services or the grocery store.

- Sharing some vegetables from your garden with those who cannot grow their own.

- Buying a meal at a restaurant for someone who cannot afford to do so for you in return.

- Sharing some extra canned goods with a family that needs them much more.

- Serving a neighbor by mowing their yard or babysitting so they can have a date.

- Changing a flat tire for someone stranded on the road.

- Serving a senior citizen who needs chores done around their home.

- Being there to help or maybe just to listen.

- Giving food to the hungry, drink to the thirsty, shelter to a stranger, clothing to the naked, medicine to the sick and visiting those in prison (Matthew 25:31-46).

Conclusion

Much of this is summarized by saying that a servant must be unselfish. That is probably the chief characteristic of those who truly serve. In Mark 10, James and John asked for positions of authority in the kingdom. The others didn't like that very much (verse 41). But, that was because they were certain that they, rather than the other two, deserved those important positions in which they could be served by many. Jesus reminded them and us that, no matter what you see in the world, you are considered great by God only when you, through love, serve the needs of others.

CHAPTER 3

Care for One Another

"...so that there should be no division in the body, but that its parts
should have equal concern for each other"
(1 Corinthians 12:25)

In 1 Corinthians 12:25, the apostle Paul tells the church at Corinth, and, by implication, us, that Christians are to "care for one another" (New King James Version). As we have pointed out before, the church is to be a family and, as in all families, we are to love and provide for the needs of each other. As the NIV puts it, "its parts should have equal concern for each other."

Another way to say that is to note that we are to be concerned about others and not merely about ourselves. When he was in a Roman prison, Paul sent Timothy to Philippi to check on the status of a relatively new group of disciples he had been forced to leave prematurely. "I hope in the Lord Jesus to send Timothy to you soon, that I also may be cheered when I receive news about you. I have no one else like him, who takes a genuine interest in your welfare" (Philippians 2:19-20). When Paul uses the phrase translated as "genuine interest," he is saying that Timothy legitimately cared for the Christians there in a sincere and genuine way, unlike so many others who had ulterior motives.

Paul also tells us of his own concern for the churches he had planted in various parts of the world. "Besides everything else, I face daily the pressure of my concern for all the churches" (2 Corinthians 11:28). Note that he felt that concern for his brothers and sisters in the Lord on a daily basis, not just occasionally.

Interestingly, most of the time, the Bible tells us not to take care, be concerned about, or worry about, things (see Matthew 6:25-34 and Philippians 4:6). In those places, we are told not to worry about material possessions, but rather, we are to trust God and believe that he will provide for our needs.

But, when it comes to our relationships in the kingdom of Christ, the Lord instructs us to be concerned about each other. Don't forget that this instruction was first given to the church at Corinth, a carnal, divided group of immature Christians. As proof of that, note his words in 1 Corinthians 3:1-3. "Brothers, I could not address you as spiritual but as worldly—mere infants in Christ. I gave you milk, not solid food, for you were not yet ready for it. Indeed, you are still not ready. You are still worldly. For since there is jealousy and quarreling among you, are you not worldly? Are you not acting like mere men?" They were having all kinds of problems and this letter was sent to them by the apostle to try to straighten out some of those problems.

1 Corinthians 12:25 points out that there are to be no divisions in the body of Christ. At Corinth, some were proud, even arrogant, about the spiritual gifts they had been given by God. They thought themselves better than others. Others were jealous and bitter that their gifts were less significant, in their own eyes, and that made them less important. He is showing them, and us, that there is no room for envy, strife, greed, pride, feelings of inferiority, and discord in the Lord's church.

Notice a series of passages from the New Testament which apply to this "one another" responsibility to be concerned about each other.

In Acts 4:32-37, we read of those who shared some of their physical possessions with others because they cared about each other. Barnabas is singled out, because of the great heart he had for others, but he was by no means the only one helping others. "All the believers were one in heart and mind. No one claimed that any of his possessions was his own, but they shared everything they had. With great power the apostles continued to testify to the resurrection of the Lord Jesus, and much grace was upon them all. There were no needy persons among them. For from time to time those who owned lands or houses sold them, brought the money from the sales and put it at the apostles' feet, and it was distributed to anyone as he had need. Joseph, a Levite from Cyprus, whom the apostles called Barnabas (which means Son of Encouragement), sold a field he owned and brought the money and put it at the apostles' feet." It was not "every man for himself." It was a clear matter of love and concern for others that led them to make great sacrifices so willingly and freely.

In Acts 6:1-6, we see an episode in which the Grecian widows were being neglected. The context would clearly indicate that this was an oversight due to the heavy work load put on the apostles. When this situation was brought to their attention, they immediately remedied the circumstance and met the needs of those who were more vulnerable and needed others to care for them.

Romans 12:15 says this: "Rejoice with those who rejoice; mourn with those who mourn." This shows us the importance of sharing mutual feelings of joy and sorrow. It indicates a closeness of life and heart to know such situations and to react in a way that would be appropriate to the need.

"If anyone considers himself to be religious and yet does not keep a tight rein on his tongue, he deceives himself and his religion is worthless. Religion that God our Father accepts as pure and faultless is this: to look after orphans and widows in their distress and to keep oneself from being polluted by the world" (James 1:26-27). Much emphasis is put in sermons and Bible classes on the need to keep our lives pure and unspotted by the world, but James places equal importance on looking after the necessities of the unfortunate, those who are not in position to help themselves and who will be unable to return the favor. We need to "visit" (NKJV) them and provide for their needs, because we are to be a people who have sincere concern for others.

One notable example from the Old Testament should make this point also. In Ecclesiastes 4:9-12, the Preacher taught us this important principle about being there for each other. "Two are better than one, because they have a good return for their work: If one falls down, his friend can help him up. But pity the man who falls and has no one to help him up! Also, if two lie down together, they will keep warm. But how can one keep warm alone? Though one may be overpowered, two can defend themselves. A cord of three strands is not quickly broken." It is vital that Christians help each other, even when times are hard. Perhaps, especially when times are hard.

Bearing One Another's Burdens

A similar duty to caring for others is found in the passage that teaches us to bear each other's burdens. "Brothers, if someone is caught in a sin, you who are spiritual should restore him gently. But watch yourself, or you also may be tempted. Carry each other's burdens, and in this way you will fulfill the law of Christ" (Galatians 6:1-2).

In the immediate context, he is talking about the burdens of sin. He follows up the teaching of Galatians, chapter 5 about the battle between the works of the flesh and the fruit of the Spirit in the life of each individual, with a warning (6:1) that even Christians can be overtaken with ungodliness. Those who are spiritually minded are to help their brothers and sisters to be restored to the Lord when they have been weak and have stumbled. This is surely one of the most difficult tasks that God has asked of us.

But, there is also a broader application of this principle. We are to help one another (because, in the body, "its parts should have equal concern for each other") to carry or bear any burden of life that may be wearing others down.

Examples of Bearing One Another's Burdens

- those who are having marital difficulties

- a family that has lost their home through foreclosure

- parents whose children are rebelling

- young people who are having a hard time maintaining sexual purity

- those who are struggling in school

- those who are lonely, depressed, upset, or discouraged

- one who has just lost a job

- those who are stuck in a job they hate

- one who has experienced a death in the family

- one who is burdened with a chronic illness

- those who are wrestling with drug or alcohol addiction

- those struggling with depression

- those whose friends have let them down

There are so many people who are wearing down under life's burdens. They have, in many cases, shown themselves to be unable to overcome those tests alone. It therefore becomes our responsibility, as their brothers and sisters, to help them to lift that load and take one more step with God.

Friends in Proverbs

Much of what we have discussed in this chapter could be summarized by saying that we are to be best friends to each other. Take note of these passages about the importance of friendship from the book of Proverbs. Several of the verses speak of the significance of choosing the right kind of friends, while others remind us of our duty to be the right kind of friend for others.

"My son, if sinners entice you, do not give in to them. If they say, 'Come along with us; let's lie in wait for someone's blood, let's waylay some harmless soul; let's swallow them alive, like the grave, and whole, like those who go down to the pit; we will get all sorts of valuable things and fill our houses with plunder; throw in your lot with us, and we will share a common purse'—my son, do not go along with them, do not set foot on their paths; for their feet rush into sin, they are swift to shed blood" (1:10-18).

"A righteous man is cautious in friendship, but the way of the wicked leads them astray" (12:26).

"He who walks with the wise grows wise, but a companion of fools suffers harm" (13:20).

"A friend loves at all times, and a brother is born for adversity" (17:17).

"A man of many companions may come to ruin, but there is a friend who sticks closer than a brother" (18:24).

"A man who has friends must himself be friendly, But there is a friend who sticks closer than a brother" (18:24, NKJV).

"Do not make friends with a hot-tempered man, do not associate with one easily angered, or you may learn his ways and get yourself ensnared" (22:24-25).

"Wounds from a friend can be trusted, but an enemy multiplies kisses" (27:6).

"As iron sharpens iron, so one man sharpens another" (27:17).

Friends are one of the greatest treasures in life. No one may count himself poor if he has the love and affection of good friends. Enduring friendships are a key ingredient to a life well-lived.

Here is a definition of a friend by an unknown author.

> "What is a friend? I'll tell you. A friend is a person with whom you dare to be yourself. Your soul can go naked with him. He seems to ask you to put on nothing, but to be what you really are. When you are with him, you do not have to be on your guard. You can say what you think, so long as it is genuinely you. He understands those contradictions in your nature that cause others to misjudge you. With him you breathe freely. He understands. You may weep with him, laugh with him, pray with him, and through and underneath it all, he sees, knows, and loves you. A friend, I repeat, is one with whom you dare to be yourself."

Isn't that good? Isn't that the kind of friend we all want? Isn't that the kind of friend we ought to be for one another?

My wife, Lisa, has a plaque which quotes this Arabian proverb. "A friend is one to whom one may pour out all the contents of one's heart, chaff and wheat together, knowing that the gentlest of hands will take and sift it; keeping what is worth keeping and, with a breath of kindness, blow the rest away." Let me say it one more time. Isn't that the kind of friend we seek and ought to be?

Conclusion

Care for one another. Be concerned about the needs, feelings, emotions and perceptions of others. Love and be loved. Serve and be served. Help one another on the uneven road of life. Help one another to have a relationship with God. Are you fulfilling your part of these "one another" responsibilities?

CHAPTER 4

Encourage One Another

"Therefore encourage one another and build each other up,
just as in fact you are doing."
(1 Thessalonians 5:11)

One of my favorite passages is Galatians 6:9. I read it often, especially when I need some encouragement. It says: "Let us not become weary in doing good, for at the proper time we will reap a harvest if we do not give up." That is so helpful to me. I must admit that, at times, I grow discouraged and feel like giving up. There are times when I just need a "shot in the arm" to keep me going. And sometimes, simply reading an uplifting passage like this one is all I need.

However, I readily admit that there are times when I need more. There are times when I need the encouragement that can only come from another disciple who lifts me up and gives me the strength I need. This chapter is going to discuss the responsibility we all have to "encourage one another and build up each other."

The Son of Encouragement

His name was Joseph (or Joses, in some translations). But the apostles changed his name, giving him a "nickname" that fit his character and attitude of life. They called him Barnabas, which means "Son of Encouragement." What a name! Many people might be called "Grumpy" or "Lefty" or "Sourpuss." (I saw an obituary in the local paper the other day that listed a deceased man's nickname as "Wino." His family must have been so proud.) But how many people do you know who are so encouraging to others that they could be called a son or daughter of encouragement?

Let's examine a series of passages about Barnabas including Acts 4:32-37, where he received his new name:

> "All the believers were one in heart and mind. No one claimed that any of his possessions was his own, but they shared everything they had. With great power the apostles continued to testify to the resurrection of the Lord Jesus, and much grace was upon them all. There were no needy persons among them. For from time to time those who owned lands or houses sold them, brought the money from the sales and put it at the apostles' feet, and it was distributed to anyone as he had need.
>
> Joseph, a Levite from Cyprus, whom the apostles called Barnabas (which means Son of Encouragement), sold a field he owned and brought the money and put it at the apostles' feet."

Apparently, he was a man of considerable wealth. He owned a field, was from Cyprus, but lived in Jerusalem. (Or at least, he had lived there since Pentecost. He may well have been one of the 3000 who became Christians in Acts 2:41.) But when the situation became difficult for some of the new disciples, other disciples sold possessions to help them. It is clear that many Christians did this. But, for some reason, Barnabas is singled out and mentioned by the Holy Spirit. Maybe his gift was the largest single offering. Maybe he was able to help more Christians with what he had than others. Maybe he is just going to be mentioned later in the book of Acts and this was Luke's way of introducing him to us. At any rate, it is clear from what is said that Barnabas' generosity was merely an extension of his character and personality. It was not this act alone that led the apostles to change his name. It was his overall lifestyle and devotion to the Lord's cause that resulted in his being called, as the old King James says it, the son of consolation. He encouraged others to be faithful to God and so, they simply called him what he was—"the Son of Encouragement."

And from that point on, he is always referred to in the Bible as Barnabas, never again as Joseph. This episode is only one of many. Acts 9:26-28 tells us more:

> "When he (Saul) came to Jerusalem, he tried to join the disciples, but they were all afraid of him, not believing that he really was a disciple. But Barnabas took him and brought him to the apostles. He told them how Saul on his journey had seen the Lord and that the Lord had spoken to him, and how in Damascus he had preached fearlessly in the name of Jesus. So Saul stayed with them and moved about freely in Jerusalem, speaking boldly in the name of the Lord."

If you can, just try to imagine how frightened they must have been of Saul of Tarsus, and for good reason. He had been a threat to their personal lives, to the stability of the church and to spread of the gospel of Christ. Acts, chapter 9, starts out with these words. "Meanwhile, Saul was still breathing out murderous threats against the Lord's disciples. He went to the high priest and asked him for letters to the synagogues in Damascus, so that if he found any there who belonged to the Way, whether men or women, he might take them as prisoners to Jerusalem" (verses 1-2). That was the Saul of Tarsus who had left Jerusalem and, now, he has returned, claims to be one of them and wants to join the fellowship of believers. It is very easy to understand that they were convinced it was merely some sort of trick, a clever move to infiltrate their number, gain insider information about their membership and use that to destroy them. They were naturally reluctant to accept him at face value.

But then, the Son of Encouragement enters the picture. He stands up for Saul when everyone else is afraid of him. He defends him when everyone wants to exclude him. Barnabas believed that Saul's conversion was legitimate and that, as Christians, they needed to embrace him, welcome him and begin to use his abundant talents. With that endorsement, the church accepted the former persecutor. Here we see the results of that decision. "Then the church throughout Judea, Galilee and Samaria enjoyed a time of peace. It was strengthened; and encouraged by the Holy Spirit, it grew in numbers, living in the fear of the Lord" (verse 31). Much of that success and numerical growth started when Barnabas encouraged the Jerusalem church to accept Saul. Look at what Acts 11:19-26 records:

> "Now those who had been scattered by the persecution in connection with Stephen traveled as far as Phoenicia, Cyprus and Antioch, telling the message only to Jews. Some of them, however, men from Cyprus and Cyrene, went to Antioch and began to speak to Greeks also, telling them the good news about the Lord Jesus. The Lord's hand was with them, and a great number of people believed and turned to the Lord. News of this reached the ears of the church at Jerusalem, and they sent Barnabas to Antioch. When he arrived and saw the evidence of the grace of God, he was glad and encouraged them all to remain true to the Lord with all their hearts. He was a good man, full of the Holy Spirit and faith, and a great number of people were brought to the Lord. Then Barnabas went to Tarsus to look for Saul, and when he found him, he brought him to Antioch. So for a whole year Barnabas and Saul met with the church and taught great numbers of people. The disciples were called Christians first at Antioch."

The book of Acts records the spread of the gospel of Christ throughout the known world. Acts 10 and 11 tell us of the early stages of taking the good news to Gentiles, not merely to the Jews. Those who had been forced to leave their homes during the intense persecution of the Jerusalem Christians, rather than giving up their faith, were determined to spread the message of salvation wherever they went (Acts 8:4). Philip went to Samaria, to a desert road in Gaza, to Azotus and then to Caesarea. Simon Peter went to the household of Cornelius, the first Gentile converts. Others took the gospel to Phoenicia, Cyprus and Antioch and many were converted to the Lord, both Jews and Greeks. When the apostles heard that there was a new church in Antioch, comprised, of course, of all new disciples, they wanted to send someone there who could really strengthen and uplift them. As they looked in their midst to find one suited for the task, one name stood out—Barnabas. Who else? No doubt, there were others who could have done a good job. But one preacher would best meet their needs, the Son of Encouragement. So they sent Barnabas and he went to Antioch. The text says, "When he arrived and saw the evidence of the grace of God, he was glad and encouraged them all to remain true to the Lord with all their hearts."

Did you notice the description of Barnabas found in the passage? It says, "He was a good man, full of the Holy Spirit and faith" and tells us that, as a result of the good work he did there, "a great number of people were brought to the Lord." Barnabas was not just an encourager of fellow disciples, but also one who encouraged the lost to come to the cross of Christ and be saved. And many were saved through his efforts. So many, apparently, that he felt overwhelmed by the size of the work that needed to be done and, therefore, he left briefly and went to get his old friend, Saul of Tarsus, to help him with the work. They worked side by side "for a whole year." (Wow, wouldn't that be great to attend a church with two evangelists like Barnabas and Paul!) They "met with the church and taught great numbers of people." And, it was during this period of encouragement and great numerical and spiritual growth that "the disciples were called Christians first at Antioch." What a privilege—to be the first disciples divinely referred to by their new name, the name of their Savior and Lord! Right at the heart of all of that growth was "the Son of Encouragement." Can you see that, wherever he went, he uplifted others? That's what God wants all of us to do for each other.

Let's notice in Acts 15:36-40, one more example of Barnabas at work.

> "Some time later Paul said to Barnabas, 'Let us go back and visit the brothers in all the towns where we preached the word of the Lord and see how they are doing.' Barnabas wanted to take John, also called Mark, with them, but Paul did not think it wise to take him, because he had deserted them in Pamphylia and had not continued with them in the work. They had such a sharp disagreement that they parted company. Barnabas took Mark and sailed for Cyprus, but Paul chose Silas and left, commended by the brothers to the grace of the Lord. He went through Syria and Cilicia, strengthening the churches."

It was true that John Mark had left the first journey early (Acts 13:13). There could be many explanations for that, but they would all be speculative.

Why it happened is not as significant as the fact that it did happen. But, when it was time to return and check on the spiritual progress of the churches, Barnabas wanted to give Mark a second chance and Paul did not want to do so. The contention was so sharp that they split up and went different directions. (Interestingly enough, that meant that more people probably were helped than if they had stayed together.) To this day, Christians have discussed this situation and what ought to have been done. Some think Paul was right because he was "commended by the brothers to the grace of God" and the text continues with his journey. Others feel that this should not be interpreted as meaning that Barnabas was wrong and have felt his was the more godly action. Only God knows for sure. But, one thing stands out. Barnabas wanted to encourage John Mark and was unwilling to give up on him. That shouldn't surprise us, should it? That was his nature. That was just the kind of edifying Christian he was. (Years later, Paul and Mark had been reconciled and were again working side by side—Colossians 4:10. This passage also tells us that Barnabas and Mark were related to one another, perhaps a further explanation for his willingness to go the extra mile with John Mark.)

The Goal

Our goal in all of this is to build each other up and make each of us stronger as Christians. We are supposed to help each other make it to heaven. Therefore, whatever we do, everything must be done with the goal of helping one another to be more pleasing to God.

The main "tool" God has given us to help in this encouragement business is the Bible. When Paul was leaving the Ephesian elders and wanted to say one more thing that would help them, he said this. "Now I commit you to God and to the word of his grace, which can build you up and give you an inheritance among all those who are sanctified" (Acts 20:32). One of the most important things we can do to edify each other is to conduct and faithfully attend Bible classes, led by challenging and encouraging Bible teachers who love the Lord.

I grew up in a small town church and was taken regularly to Bible classes all my life. I had many different teachers from various backgrounds but one thing stood out. They loved the Lord and wanted me and the others in the class to grow up to love him also. They had little formal education, their grammar wasn't always perfect and they weren't up-to-date on the latest educational techniques. But I had no doubt that God was first in their life and they wanted to instill that same kind of commitment in me. I shall be eternally grateful for the spiritual encouragement I received from these godly men and women.

Our Words

Much of the building up we do of each other is done by the words we speak. We need to be careful to realize that our words have great power for good or evil, depending on how we direct them. The slightest thing said to someone else can have an eternal impact for good or bad. The book of Proverbs teaches us to be aware of the power of the spoken word in our interactions with others. Notice just a few of these verses.

"A man finds joy in giving an apt reply—and how good is a timely word" (Proverbs 15:23, NIV).

"A man has joy by the answer of his mouth, And a word spoken in due season, how good it is! (Proverbs 15:23, NKJV).

"Pleasant words are a honeycomb, sweet to the soul and healing to the bones"(Proverbs 15:24).

"A word aptly spoken is like apples of gold in settings of silver" (Proverbs 25:11).

"As iron sharpens iron, so one man sharpens another" (Proverbs 27:17).

Practical Applications

What are some ways we can encourage others? How can we put this important principle into action?

- Send another disciple a card, thank you note or a small gift. And do so at totally unexpected times, not just on birthdays or anniversaries.

- Pick up the telephone and call someone, just to say "thanks" or to express your appreciation for something he or she has done.

- Have a warm, positive atmosphere and attitude in all you do. This reflects appreciation for people and for the blessings you have received from God.

- Don't feel like you have to criticize others even if you disapprove of something they said, or how they dressed or the music they listened to. (I don't mean we should overlook sin in peoples' lives, but we are not to judge people in areas of opinion just because their judgment about something is different from ours. This applies to our own children as well as others. Someone has said that our children need models, not critics.)

- Be supportive and uplifting, especially when you know that others are hurting. That's when they need us the most.

- Make a list of people you know and their specific needs. Expand the list as you become aware of additional situations. Then ask yourself regularly, "What can I do today to help one person on my list?"

- Express your love for others with a word of encouragement. Challenge them to stretch themselves and to do something they have never tried before. Tell them "I know you can do it" and tell them why you think they can.

- Stay aware and be thinking about this. Intentionally help others. Because this takes time, energy and thoughtfulness, it often doesn't come naturally. Therefore, consciously make an effort to continue to do this.

Discouragement

Let's now think for a moment about the opposite idea— discouraging one another. What would be some examples of things we might do that would tear others down spiritually, rather than uplift?

- Saying derogatory, hurtful things without thinking.

- Simply ignoring Christians in the fellowship...late to worship service and the first to leave.

- Assuming the worst about others and then treating them poorly based on an incorrect assumption.

- Gossiping.

- Setting a bad example for others to follow, rather than modeling genuine commitment and devotion.

- Throwing some cold water on a new idea someone else has.

Daily Contact

One of the reasons we don't encourage others as we should is that we often are not in touch with each other enough. I get the impression from reading the New Testament that the first Christians spent a lot more social time together (away from the collective worship services) than we do today. We sometimes just aren't around other Christians enough to encourage them as we should.

"Every day they continued to meet together in the temple courts. They broke bread in their homes and ate together with glad and sincere hearts, praising God and enjoying the favor of all the people. And the Lord added to their number ("to the church," NKJV) daily those who were being saved" (Acts 2:46-47). Did you see that? They met together in the temple courts for public periods of worship and instruction (in "the apostles' teaching"—verse 42). But they also met daily in their homes for meals and mutual edification. The result was that the church was being increased in number on a daily basis. Maybe the reason more churches aren't growing, especially on a daily basis, is that the disciples are not spending time together day by day.

When some Christians were in danger of returning to the Law of Moses and abandoning the gospel of Christ, God inspired the book of Hebrews to help them remain faithful. He revealed to them what a true life of faith was and reminded them that what they had now in the gospel is "better" than what they had under the old law. As a part of that teaching, the writer said this, "See to it, brothers, that none of you has a sinful, unbelieving heart that turns away from the living God. But encourage one another daily, so long as it is called Today, so that none of you may be hardened by sin's deceitfulness" (Hebrews 3:12-13). One of the "safety nets" that God has built into the Christian system is the constant (note that the Bible says "daily") contact with fellow believers and the spiritual encouragement and help that will naturally result from this regular time spent together. More Christians would stay faithful if we spent more time together, lifting each other up and encouraging one another to greater commitment and devotion to God.

Conclusion

There are numerous verses in the New Testament that point to this kind of help we are to give each other. Many of those verses use different words like, comfort, exhort, admonish, and edify each other. It isn't always easy to be a faithful Christian. We need help from time to time. God has put us into each other's lives to be there for one another and to help each other make it to heaven. I'm reminded of the words about Paul and Barnabas as they neared the end of the first missionary journey. "They preached the good news in that city and won a large number of disciples. Then they returned to Lystra, Iconium and Antioch, strengthening the disciples and encouraging them to remain true to the faith" (Acts 14:21-22a). Let's strengthen one another and encourage each other to remain faithful to our Master that we might spend eternity together in his holy presence. Amen!

CHAPTER 5

Greet One Another

"All the brothers here send you greetings.
Greet one another with a holy kiss."
(1 Corinthians 16:20)

"Greet one another with a holy kiss.
All the churches of Christ send greetings."
(Romans 16:16)

In the first century, a greeting was a common way of expressing love and appreciation for others and their contributions to the cause of Christ. To greet someone was to acknowledge their worth, to welcome them, to let them know how much you loved them. It was more than a passing and meaningless, "Hi, how are you?" The old King James Version says, in most of those places, that we are to salute one another. The word, salute, carries with it the idea of respect for others that is included in the greeting.

Although it is quite long and contains several unfamiliar names that are difficult to pronounce, please notice Romans 16:3-16.

"Greet Priscilla and Aquila, my fellow workers in Christ Jesus. They risked their lives for me. Not only I but all the churches of the Gentiles are grateful to them.

Greet also the church that meets at their house.

Greet my dear friend Epenetus, who was the first convert to Christ in the province of Asia.

Greet Mary, who worked very hard for you.

Greet Adronicus and Junias, my relatives who have been in prison with me. They are outstanding among the apostles, and they were in Christ before I was.

Greet Ampliatus, whom I love in the Lord.

Greet Urbanus, our fellow worker in Christ, and my dear friend Stachys.

Greet Apelles, tested and approved in Christ.

Greet those who belong to the household of Aristobulus.

Greet Herodion, my relative.

Greet those in the household of Narcissus who are in the Lord.

Greet Tryphena and Tryphosa, those women who work hard in the Lord.

Greet my dear friend Persis, another woman who has worked very hard in the Lord.

Greet Rufus, chosen in the Lord, and his mother, who has been a mother to me too.

Greet Asyncritus, Phlegon, Hermes, Patrobas, Hermas and the brothers with them.

Greet Philologus, Julia, Nereus and his sister, and Olympas and all the saints with them.

Greet one another with a holy kiss. All the churches of Christ send greetings."

Paul "greets" approximately twenty six people by name, along with others who are unnamed (the church that meets at their house, Rufus' mother, etc).

After writing these twenty six or more personal greetings, Paul then sends greetings from several others in Corinth to those in Rome.

"Timothy, my fellow worker, sends his greetings to you, as do Lucius, Jason and Sosipater, my relatives. I, Tertius, who wrote down this letter, greet you in the Lord.

Gaius, whose hospitality I and the whole church here enjoy, sends you his greetings.

Erastus, who is the city's director of public works, and our brother Quartus send you their greetings" (verses 21-23).

Can you believe how many times the words "greet" and "greetings" are found in these verses? That should show us the importance of this to God as he inspired the Holy Spirit to include all of these personal greetings between Christians.

There are many other verses in which the New Testament emphasizes this idea of greeting others. Let's just notice a few of them.

"Greet all the saints in Christ Jesus. The brothers who are with me send greetings. All the saints send you greetings, especially those who belong to Caesar's household" (Philippians 4:22-23).

"Give my greetings to the brothers at Laodicea, and to Nympha and the church in her house" (Colossians 4:15).

"Everyone with me sends you greetings. Greet those who love us in the faith. Grace be with you all" (Titus 3:15).

"Greet all your leaders and all God's people. Those from Italy send you their greetings" (Hebrews 13:24).

"I have much to write you, but I do not want to do so with pen and ink. I hope to see you soon, and we will talk face to face. Peace to you. The friends here send their greetings. Greet the friends there by name" (3 John 13-14).

Did you realize there would be so many references to the idea of "greeting" others? It is mentioned more times than I would ever have dreamed. The important question we must ask ourselves, in view of this biblical emphasis, is "How seriously do we take the greeting of others?"

The Holy Kiss?

This is the part of the command that gives us the most trouble and is perhaps the reason we have essentially ignored the importance of how we greet others. We rapidly dismiss the "holy kiss" as being simply a cultural reflection of the times which has no significance for today and that's that. But let's think about it for a moment.

In the first century, kissing was (and still is, in many cultures) a common form of both greeting and telling others goodbye. In that sense, it is kind of like the word "aloha" which, in Hawaii, means both hello and farewell. We still do the same thing in groups in which we feel especially close. Families, especially, will greet one another and tell one another goodbye with a kiss, a hug, or both. It is a natural thing to do, there is absolutely nothing sexual or perverse about it, and everyone feels comfortable doing it. Close friends often feel it is appropriate to express love and affection for each other in that way. Even heads of state from many countries will treat one another in that way and may even do the same for visiting heads of state.

Would it, therefore, be wrong for Christians to practice such a greeting today—with a sincere kiss on the cheek, with nothing sexual implied or intended, or with a hug of appreciation?

The Specific or the Principle?

Is Paul, in these many passages, binding the specific method of greeting with a holy kiss? Or is he simply telling them that, when they greeted one another (in the way that was most commonly practiced then), it was to be holy and from a heart of love? I believe it to be the latter.

It seems to me, in many ways, to be parallel to the teaching in John 13:1-17, which we have already discussed in Chapter Two. He was not binding the practice of footwashing on the church for all time. He was using a common illustration of humility and service for others and tells us that we need to be humble and serve our fellow Christians.

In the same way, he is not requiring us to greet one another in an artificial or unnatural way. He is telling us to show that we care for one another and love one another in our sincere, heart-felt greeting of others.

The *Holy* Kiss?

When he uses the word "holy" to describe this kiss, he is saying that our greetings of one another should be sincere, pure, genuine and godly. The opposite of that would be greetings that are vain or empty.

Outside of the passages we have already noticed, there are three examples of kisses in the New Testament.

1. Jesus and Judas

"While he was still speaking, Judas, one of the Twelve, arrived. With him was a large crowd armed with swords and clubs, sent from the chief priests and elders of the people. Now the betrayer has arranged a signal with them: 'The one I kiss is the man; arrest him.' Going at once to Jesus, Judas said, 'Greetings, Rabbi!' and kissed him" (Matthew 26:47-49).

Clearly, this was not a holy kiss. It was a kiss of betrayal, the exact opposite of what a holy kiss ought to be. It was used merely as a signal of identification that would point out to the armed mob which of the men present was the one they had come to apprehend. But, even with that, it is obvious that this was a familiar greeting between the Rabbi and his students. Judas and the other disciples had, no doubt, greeted Jesus with a kiss often and so, it was not out of place here. He chose such a signal because it was their common greeting. It was his motive on this occasion that made this an unholy kiss.

2. Father and the Prodigal Son

"So he got up and went to his father. But while he was still a long way off, his father saw him and was filled with compassion for him; he ran to his son, threw his arms around him and kissed him" (Luke 15:20; read verses 11-32 for the larger context).

The son had left home under bad circumstances. He had been immoral, ungodly and profligate. He had now hit bottom and had nowhere else to turn. So he returned home to his father. And, unlike so many today, the father welcomed his son home with dignity and respect. Because of the tremendous joy he felt at his son's return, he ran to meet him, threw his arms around him in love and welcomed him back with a holy kiss. It was genuine and loving; it was truly an embracing kiss that said, "I love you and I am so glad you've come back home."

3. Paul and the Ephesian Elders

"When he had said this, he knelt down with all of them and prayed. They all wept as they embraced him and kissed him. What grieved them most was his statement that they would never see his face again. Then they accompanied him to the ship" (Acts 20:36-38).

Paul had spent three years of his life establishing and working with this church (Acts 19; Acts 20:31). He knew this joyous reunion would probably be the last time they spent together on the earthly side of eternity and that, when they parted, they would see each other no more. They prayed together. They embraced one another. And they parted from one another with a holy kiss. It expressed their appreciation for each other, in both directions. They appreciated all that Paul had done for them; they wanted him to know that they felt the same. And so, they kissed one another as they said goodbye.

Conclusion

Think with me of some situations you may have found yourself in from time-to-time. Think about the difference in what we might say with how we really feel.

"Hi. How are you doing?" (Oh no, I really hope they don't tell me—they always drag me down with their problems.)

"We are so glad to have you visit our services today." (This is said to a visitor while you are already thinking about getting out of the building quickly so you can beat everyone to the local restaurant.)

"Thanks for calling. It's great to hear from you." (I hope you don't call again, I've got better things to do.)

"It's so good to see you." (I hate seeing this guy.)

Now, be honest. Have you ever felt that way? Have you ever put on a false front and pretended to be so happy to see someone when really you were not? I would not suggest that we be rude to such people and let them know that we are not glad to be around them, but that we work on our attitude of love and affection for others so that we can legitimately greet them with love and respect.

As many times as it is mentioned in the Bible, this is obviously important to the Lord. We need to make certain that it is important to us also and that we greet one another in a way that would communicate our love and glorify our Father in heaven.

CHAPTER 6

Honor One Another

"Love must be sincere. Hate what is evil; cling to what is good.
Be devoted to one another in brotherly love.
Honor one another above yourselves."
(Romans 12:9-10)

The apostle Paul wrote these words to the church in Rome. "Give everyone what you owe him: If you owe taxes, pay taxes; if revenue, then revenue; if respect, then respect; if honor, then honor" (Romans 13:7). The idea of giving honor to others stems from the mutual respect that we are to have for each other as fellow disciples of Christ. We are to esteem them or respect them as those who have value. This ties in with the idea that all Christians are equal before God. He knows that. It is our responsibility to make certain that we understand that principle as well.

God's Honor Roll

There are numerous people to whom the Bible teaches us that we must give honor or respect. Here are a dozen scriptures about this subject as we look at *who* we are to honor and then *how* we are to show honor to these.

1. John 5:22-23—"Moreover, the Father judges no one, but has entrusted all judgment to the Son, that all may honor the Son just as they honor the Father. He who does not honor the Son does not honor the Father, who sent him."

We honor and glorify God when we do those things he teaches in his word. As several have pointed out over the years, God gives us commandments, not suggestions. We also honor God when we honor his Son. Jesus is the Son of God, false teaching about his nature and deity notwithstanding, and all who would dishonor him do the same for the Father. It's a package deal. You can't blaspheme one without blaspheming the other. You cannot claim to worship one while, at the same time, speaking against the other.

Somehow the idea of obeying God has fallen out of favor in many religious circles. False ideas about the grace of God have led many to believe that man is no participant at all in salvation. It is true enough that no person can earn or merit his own salvation. But, it is equally true that God expects us to obey him and his word. Jesus taught, "Not everyone who says to me, 'Lord, Lord,' will enter the kingdom of heaven, but only he who does the will of my Father who is in heaven" (Matthew 7:21). Christ is also described as "the source of eternal salvation for all who obey him" (Hebrews 5:9). The Lord also said this: "There is a judge for the one who rejects me and does not accept my words; that very word which I spoke will condemn him at the last day" (John 12:48). God did not reveal to us his word through the inspiration of the Holy Spirit and warn us that we will be judged by it only to tell us that we do not have to do what that word says. We honor God by our obedience to the Bible; we dishonor him and Christ when we reject the inspired word.

2. Romans 12:10—"Be devoted to one another in brotherly love. Honor one another above yourselves."

This passage speaks of the importance of having the proper respect for our fellow disciples. All too often, we are quite good at spotting the flaws in one another. We all have them. Some are just more obvious than others (that's really the point of 1 Timothy 5:24-25). It really doesn't take too long to find the faults in others. Those who "major" in critiquing and criticizing others need to realize that we all have good points as well. And our duty to each other includes having an appreciation for the uniqueness and abilities of others, no matter what they might be. Being devoted to one another in brotherly love means that we have a special bond with our fellow Christians that we just don't have with those outside of God's family. There should be a closeness that transcends differences and that overlooks weaknesses and mistakes others make (that doesn't mean we should ignore sin in another's life, but that we should lovingly help others to overcome those problems).

The New King James Version renders the verse this way: "Be kindly affectionate to one another with brotherly love, in honor giving preference to one another." The first phrase indicates the affection that we should have for our fellow disciples. The second phrase emphasizes that we must show deference to others in areas where we do not always agree. To honor another is to give his or her opinions and views the respect they deserve, even in times when we believe another judgment ought to prevail. The foundation of such considerate treatment of others is "brotherly love."

3. 1 Corinthians 12:22-24—"On the contrary, those parts of the body that seem to be weaker are indispensable, and the parts that we think are less honorable we treat with special honor. And the parts that are unpresentable are treated with special modesty."

These verses acknowledge that there are different levels of spiritual maturity within every local church. There will always be those of great maturity and those who are babes in Christ. Paul is dealing in this passage with how we are treat those who are weaker spiritually and he says they are to be given honor, special honor. They must never be ridiculed or made to feel unimportant to the body. They must be made to feel valuable and important and how we treat them must contribute to that sense of worth. They must understand that we are glad to have them as members of our church family in the Lord and know that we value their contributions to the Lord's work, at their level of participation. Maybe in time, their talents will increase. If so, great. But we need to realize that there will be some who simply never grow as they should. We need to treat them with respect and honor, not disdain, and do nothing that would damage their fragile relationship with God.

4. 1 Corinthians 12:26—"If one part suffers, every part suffers with it; if one part is honored, every part rejoices with it."

The first part of that verse is relatively easy. When something happens that causes another Christian sorrow, we rally around that one and help to ease the pain. It may be a death in the family, a serious illness, a rebellious child, or any number of things that can break the heart. Whatever it is that causes the hurt, disciples should be there to help ease the pain. And I think we are, for the most part.

But, it seems to be a little more difficult, in some ways, to rejoice with those who rejoice. Sometimes the success of another brings out feelings of jealousy or envy rather than jubilation. Many times, we think it should be us enjoying the success and it can be hard to give credit where credit is due, when it's due to someone else. That just ought not to be so. We should be grateful for every good thing that happens to others and such success and honor should be met with excitement and joy.

5. Ephesians 6:2-3—"'Honor your father and mother'—which is the first commandment with a promise—that it may go well with you and that you may enjoy long life on the earth."

We've heard this one all our lives, right? Honor and obey your parents. Do what they say. Show them respect. How are we doing carrying out such responsibilities to our parents?

This is one of those things that seems to be easier as we grow older. As we ourselves mature, it becomes much more natural to grow in our respect for our parents. But, no matter how old we might be, even teenagers and those who are younger need to honor and respect their parents.

Someone said that, no matter how aggravating we may consider our parents to be right now, we will miss them terribly when they are gone. I think that's right. Those who have lost their parents, in most cases (there are exceptions, of course), would give almost anything to have one more day or simply one more conversation with them. Those who have not lost their parents should probably learn from that, before it's too late.

As verse one points out, we honor our parents by obeying them. The dynamics of honoring change as our circumstances change. When we marry, we "leave father and mother" to be joined to our spouse. But the honor and reverence that we ought to have for them should remain.

6. 1 Timothy 1:17—"Now to the King eternal, immortal, invisible, the only God, be honor and glory for ever and ever. Amen."

This passage again points out the One who is deserving of all ultimate honor: God, our king, our creator, our heavenly father. He is the eternal one. He is the one in whose being dwells immortality. He is the one who ought to receive all honor and glory "for ever and ever." It would not be possible to be too reverent when it comes to God. It would not be possible to over-obey him. He must be first in all that we do. And everything we do must be done in a way that would bring honor and glory to him. "So whether you eat or drink or whatever you do, do it all for the glory of God" (1 Corinthians 10:31).

7. 1 Timothy 5:3—"Give proper recognition to (Honor, NKJV) those widows who are really in need."

In the early church, they had an unusual number of widows with tremendous material needs. They simply could not provide those needs for themselves. It therefore became incumbent upon their brothers and sisters in the Lord to meet those needs. But, as time went on, and the number of such widows increased (no doubt, in proportion to the growing number of disciples in general), there came to be some who were more needy than others. How could the church distinguish such?

First, Paul taught that family ought to take the primary responsibility to care for their own (1 Timothy 5:4, 8, 16). Then, other Christians needed to help those within their realm of opportunity. And finally, the church had an obligation to meet the needs of those "who are really in need," meaning those who had no family or other means of support. Paul even set forth qualifications for those who were to be cared for by the church on a permanent basis (1 Timothy 5:9-10). This is the "proper recognition" (NIV) or "honor" (NKJV) that he refers to in the above verse. Those widows who could not care for themselves and had no one else to do so, and who had been lifelong servants of the Lord were to be given special honor by having the church provide for them.

8. 1 Timothy 5:17-18—"The elders who direct the affairs of the church well are worthy of double honor, especially those whose work is preaching and teaching. For the Scripture says, 'Do not muzzle the ox while it is treading out the grain,' and 'The worker deserves his wages.'"

Elders, in Bible times, were the spiritual leaders who, due to the knowledge and maturity that can come only with age and experience, served as spiritual shepherds for the flock in their midst, the local church. They were charged by the Lord with the awesome responsibility of directing the affairs of the church. If conflicts arose, they were to settle them (1 Corinthians 6:1-8). They were to feed, protect, encourage, teach, guide, serve, rebuke when necessary and, in general, help others who were spiritually weak. Those who did their job well (that implies that some would not do it well) were to be accorded "double honor." The first honor would be the regular respect that any mature Christian ought to get from others. The double honor, as described in the verse, would involve financial support from the church. For those who served in a "full-time" capacity, whose work was preaching and teaching, the church was to help them by paying them for their work. He quotes two passages, one from the Old Testament in Deuteronomy 25:4 and one from the New Testament in Luke 10:7, to show that God approves of such financial honor being given to shepherds who devote themselves to the Lord's work.

9. 1 Timothy 6:1—"All who are under the yoke of slavery should consider their masters worthy of full respect, so that God's name and our teaching may not be slandered."

Some Christians in the first century were slaves (see 1 Corinthians 1:26-29). There was an obvious tendency on the part of such to believe that, if their masters were disciples as well, this would guarantee their immediate freedom. No doubt, that happened on occasion. But, not in every circumstance was that the case and so, he deals with the attitude of those who would continue to work under others. He tells them that they should work hard, earn their keep, and serve even believing masters with respect and honor. "Those who have believing masters are not to show less respect for them because they are brothers. Instead, they are to serve them even better, because those who benefit from their service are believers, and dear to them. These are the things you are to teach and urge on them" (1 Timothy 6:2).

10. 2 Timothy 2:20-21—"In a large house there are articles not only of gold and silver, but also of wood and clay; some are for noble purposes and some for ignoble. If a man cleanses himself from the latter, he will be an instrument for noble purposes (a vessel for honor, NKJV), made holy, useful to the Master and prepared to do any good work."

    The emphasis in this passage is on being a godly servant of the Lord. As such, we are to cleanse ourselves from all defilement and ungodliness. When one did so, he was "useful to the Master and prepared to do any good work." This made him (or her) a servant of God worthy of honor, or as the NKJV puts it, "a vessel for honor."

11. 1 Peter 2:17—"Show proper respect to everyone: Love the brotherhood of believers, fear God, honor the king."

    Here we are taught to show proper respect to everyone. This seems to be a quality that is lacking on the part of so many in the world today. For some reason, sarcasm and disrespect are rampant. Starting in the home, extending to the classroom, and then to the workplace, people, young and old, need to be taught respect for other people and their property.

    He then emphasizes that we should also honor those in civil government, as symbolized by his warning to "honor the king." The king, here, represents all forms of governmental authority. The governing authorities have been established by God for the punishment of those who do wrong and the praise of those who do right (Romans 13:1-7). They keep order and direction in society. They fight crime and keep our streets safe. They enforce the laws of the city, state or nation and we ought to pay them their proper and due respect.

12. 1 Peter 3:7—"Husbands, in the same way be considerate as you live
    with your wives, and treat them with respect as the weaker partner
    and as heirs with you of the gracious gift of life, so that nothing will
    hinder your prayers."

    Men are to show the appropriate attitude toward their wives, to be
    considerate of them and their needs and to treat them with the respect
    which they deserve. Wives are "heirs with you of the gracious gift of
    life" and should not be treated as second class human beings. Some
    societies around the world do not have the proper respect for women.
    Neither do some men in places where they ought to know better. Men
    can be rude, inconsiderate, overbearing, insensitive, unemotional,
    uncaring, unhelpful and downright mean when it comes to their wives.
    (One man tried to justify the physical abuse of his wife by reminding
    me that the husband is the head of the wife and can, therefore, do
    whatever he wants to her. What a gross distortion of God's Word!)
    The apostle Peter tells us here that the prayers of such ungodly men
    will be hindered, that is, their relationship with God is damaged by
    their wicked treatment of their wives. Honor them and treat them
    with respect.

Seeking Honor

Having looked at these twelve passages that teach the proper recipients
of honor, it is necessary to understand that it is wrong to *seek honor* from
others. We should not do things just to receive public or individual praise
from people.

In Matthew 23:1-12, Jesus strongly condemned the Jewish religious
leaders who looked for ways to elevate themselves over others. They used
things like special clothing, the best seats at public affairs, and special
religious titles to receive honor from others. They knew they were better
than others; they wanted everyone else to realize that as well. Jesus taught
that those who were putting on such an external show were hypocrites and
condemned them harshly. They wanted praise; Jesus gave them criticism.
He concluded by saying, "For whoever exalts himself will be humbled,
and whoever humbles himself will be exalted."

In Mark 9:33-37, the disciples argued about which of them was the greatest. They meant that in terms of who would have the most power and influence over others. Jesus showed them that they should serve others to be considered truly great, by God and those of spiritual discernment.

The Messiah taught, "I do not accept praise from men, but I know you. I know that you do not have the love of God in your hearts. I have come in my Father's name, and you do not accept me; but if someone else comes in his own name, you will accept him. How can you believe if you accept praise from one another, yet make no effort to obtain the praise that comes from the only God?" (John 5:41-44). These are people who are more concerned with receiving honor from other people than with what God thinks of them.

The point is this. If we serve to receive honor from men, we serve in vain. If we serve because we have the love of God in our hearts and, because others appreciate our efforts, they honor us, in some way, then we serve with dignity. We shall receive honor from men and a reward from God.

Let's humbly serve God as we live together in the kingdom of the Lord. Let us seek to do his will with deep love and conviction. In so doing, let us give "honor to whom honor is due."

One Another Christianity

CHAPTER 7

Forgive One Another

"Be kind and compassionate to one another, forgiving each other,
just as in Christ God forgave you"
(Ephesians 4:32)

As Christians, we are to be possessed by a spirit or attitude of forgiveness. Mistakes and misunderstandings with each other are inevitable. People are going to say and do some things wrong that will hurt and offend us. We must be prepared to forgive others so that we might be forgiven by them when we do wrong ourselves.

In this chapter, we are going to study about the acknowledging of wrongs committed and the healing of relationships that have been damaged or strained. We will look again at biblical teaching on repentance, confession, reconciliation, restoration and forgiveness.

The principles we will talk about in this chapter can be applied to marital conflicts, parent-child differences, ill feelings toward a neighbor, but we especially want to discuss problems between Christians, including you and your preacher, Bible class teachers, elders, deacons, those who have served together on committees, or anyone else with whom you may have a spiritual disagreement and need to reconcile.

Examples of a Forgiving Spirit

Let's notice together some Bible examples of forgiveness and think about the lessons we should learn from these examples.

- Stephen

> "When they heard this, they were furious and gnashed their teeth at him. But Stephen, full of the Holy Spirit, looked up to heaven and saw the glory of God, and Jesus standing at the right hand of God. 'Look,' he said, 'I see heaven open and the Son of Man standing at the right hand of God.' At this they covered their ears and, yelling at the top of their voices, they all rushed at him, dragged him out of the city and began to stone him. Meanwhile, the witnesses laid their clothes at the feet of a young man named Saul. While they were stoning him, Stephen prayed, 'Lord Jesus, receive my spirit.' Then he fell on his knees and cried out, 'Lord, do not hold this sin against them.' When he had said this, he fell asleep" (Acts 7:54-60).

The example of forgiveness in this passage is Stephen. He is the first Christian martyr, the first one to give his life in the cause of the Messiah. On this occasion, he had just preached a historical sermon to a group of Jews, leading them up to the crucifixion, of which some of them had been a part. He tells them that they had betrayed and murdered the Son of God and that although they had received the law of God, they had not obeyed it. They became "furious" with him and completely lost control of their actions. They stoned him (can you imagine a more painful way to die?) as he called on the name of the Lord. And Stephen asked the Lord, with literally his dying breath, "Do not hold this sin against them." They were stoning him to death and he asks the Lord not to charge them with this sin! What an example of a forgiving spirit.

- Paul

> "I speak the truth in Christ—I am not lying, my conscience confirms it in the Holy Spirit—I have great sorrow and unceasing anguish in my heart. For I could wish that I myself were cursed and cut off from Christ for the sake of my brothers, those of my own race, the people of Israel" (Romans 9:1-4a).

As a former Jew who had converted to Jesus Christ, Paul was considered by the people of Israel to be a traitor. They felt him to be a real enemy and one who was a threat to the very existence of the Jewish faith. (Some people believe that's why he wrote the book of Hebrews anonymously, if he wrote it at all, so that Hebrews who had become Christians would not ignore the message from one who was thought of as a traitor.) Paul could not deny that Christ had been crucified. Nor could he deny that he had seen him alive on the road to Damascus several years later (see Acts 9). His only conclusion was that Jesus really was the Son of God as he claimed to be. He changed religions. And, from that point on, he tried to convince other Jews to do the same.

That didn't make him very popular with his former people. They resisted him at every turn and sought to discredit him so that others would not follow his example of conversion. But, as much as they opposed him, he considered himself, in many ways to be one of them. He was no longer a Jew religiously, but he still was of the Jewish race and nationally, culturally and perhaps emotionally, he felt a closeness and a bond that would never go away. And when you love someone, you want what is best for them. So, in spite of the fact that the Jewish people hated what he had become and what he was trying to do, he still wanted to convert them to Jesus Christ. He had become convinced that Jesus was the only hope of the world (John 14:6) and, he deeply wanted them to become Christians. Even though they were persecuting him, he forgave them and wanted them to accept Jesus as the Christ, the true Messiah of God.

• Jesus

> "Jesus said, 'Father, forgive them, for they do not know what they are doing'" (Luke 23:34).

Stephen and Paul were simply following the earlier example of their Master in possessing a spirit of forgiveness. Christ prayed to God, while dying on the cross, that those who were guilty of his death would be forgiven of their sins. He was willing to forgive them all, the soldiers, the thief, the Pharisees and all of those who had a part in his death.

Of course, forgiveness and pardon of sin is what the cross is all about. That's why Jesus came to the earth, lived as a man, set the perfect example and then died on the cross of Calvary. It was all so we could be forgiven by God and have the hope of eternal life in heaven. Jesus loved us so much, God loved us so deeply, that the Son of God endured the cross, despising the shame and the pain, so that we might be saved, forgiven of every trespass against his holy will.

God is a Forgiver

We must never forget that the God we serve is a forgiving God. There are so many passages that speak of his mercy, grace, love and forgiveness of mankind. Listed below are several of them. Notice, as you read these verses, the fact that God does not forgive grudgingly or with hesitation. Rather, he forgives freely and graciously, because that is his very nature.

First, notice these Old Testament passages:

- Psalms 32:1-2—"Blessed is he whose transgressions are forgiven, whose sins are covered. Blessed is the man whose sin the LORD does not count against him and in whose spirit is no deceit."

- Psalms 51:1-2—"Have mercy on me, O God, according to your unfailing love; according to your great compassion blot out my transgressions. Wash away all my iniquity and cleanse me from my sin."

- Psalms 103:2-3—"Praise the LORD, O my soul, and forget not all his benefits—who forgives all your sins and heals all your diseases."

- Psalms 103:8-14—"The LORD is compassionate and gracious, slow to anger, abounding in love. He will not always accuse, nor will he harbor his anger forever; he does not treat us as our sins deserve or repay us according to our iniquities. For as high as the heavens are above the earth, so great is his love for those who fear him; as far as the east is from the west, so far has he removed our transgressions from us. As a father has compassion on his children, so the LORD has compassion on those who fear him, for he knows how we are formed, he remembers that we are dust."

- Psalms 130:4—"But with you there is forgiveness; therefore you are feared."

- Psalms 145:8-9—"The LORD is gracious and com- passionate, slow to anger and rich in love. The LORD is good to all; he has compassion on all he has made."

- Isaiah 38:17—"Surely it was for my benefit that I suffered such anguish. In your love you kept me from the pit of destruction; you have put all my sins behind your back."

- Isaiah 43:25—"I, even I, am he who blots out your transgressions, for my own sake, and remembers your sins no more."

- Isaiah 44:22—"I have swept away your offenses like a cloud, your sins like the morning mist. Return to me, for I have redeemed you."

- Isaiah 55:6-7—"Seek the LORD while he may be found; call on him while he is near. Let the wicked forsake his way and the evil man his thoughts. Let him turn to the LORD, and he will have mercy on him, and to our God, for he will freely pardon."

- Jeremiah 3:22—"Return, faithless people; I will cure you of backsliding. Yes, we will come to you, for you are the LORD our God."

- Micah 7:18-19—"Who is a God like you, who pardons sin and forgives the transgression of the remnant of his inheritance? You do not stay angry forever but delight to show mercy. You will again have compassion on us; you will tread our sins underfoot and hurl all our iniquities into the depths of the sea."

Now, notice several verses from the New Testament. Listed below are a few of the many passages we could quote.

- John 1:29—"The next day John saw Jesus coming toward him and said, 'Look, the Lamb of God, who takes away the sin of the world!'"

- Ephesians 1:7—"In him we have redemption through his blood, the forgiveness of sins, in accordance with the riches of God's grace."

- 1 Timothy 1:15-16—"Here is a trustworthy saying that deserves full acceptance: Christ Jesus came into the world to save sinners—of whom I am the worst. But for that very reason I was shown mercy so that in me, the worst of sinners, Christ Jesus might display his unlimited patience as an example for those who would believe on him and receive eternal life."

- John 1:7- 9—"But if we walk in the light, as he is in the light, we have fellowship with one another, and the blood of Jesus, his Son, purifies us from all sin. If we claim to be without sin, we deceive ourselves and the truth is not in us. If we confess our sins, he is faithful and just and will forgive us our sins and purify us from all unrighteousness."

- Revelation 1:5—"...and from Jesus Christ, who is the faithful witness, the firstborn from the dead, and the ruler of the kings of the earth."

Isn't that impressive? God clearly wanted us to see and understand the unlimited dimensions of his forgiveness, and he inspired the Bible so that we would read over and over about his great lovingkindness. This is big time forgiveness! There is nothing we could do to deserve such mercy. What we all deserve is to be lost eternally (because "all have sinned"—Romans 3:23 and "the wages of sin is death"—Romans 6:23). That's why it's called grace. It is an undeserved gift (or, as the Bible teachers in my youth always taught me, unmerited favor) from God. God is indeed great in mercy and lovingkindness.

Examples of God's Forgiveness

I think it would be helpful for us to consider again some of the people God has forgiven. There are those in Scripture who did absolutely horrible things and the Lord forgave them of their sins. (Obviously, that should give us all hope that he will forgive us also.) Think about these cases of forgiveness.

- David (Psalm 51)

  Even though David was a man after God's own heart, he committed some grievous sins in the affair with Bathsheba. He was guilty of adultery and murder, at the very least. When Nathan the prophet confronted him with his sin, he had the same choices we all face. He could repent and ask God for pardon or he could get angry at the messenger and walk further away from the Lord. He chose the former. "Then David said to Nathan, 'I have sinned against the LORD.' Nathan replied, 'The LORD has taken away your sin. You are not going to die.'"

- Manasseh (2 Chronicles 33)

  There was no more ungodly king in the combined history of Israel and Judah than Manasseh. There was no sin which he did not commit. He was guilty of idolatry, he erected high places for pagan worship, he set up idol altars in the temple of Jehovah, he sacrificed some of his own children to heathen gods, he practiced sorcery, divination and witchcraft, he consulted mediums and spiritists, he shed much innocent blood. Literally, he did it all. But when the Assyrian army took him captive, "In his distress he sought the favor of the LORD his God and humbled himself greatly before the God of his fathers. And when he prayed to him, the LORD was moved by his entreaty and listened to his plea; so he brought him back to Jerusalem and to his kingdom. Then Manasseh knew that the LORD is God." Can you imagine that? God forgave even someone as vile and evil as Manasseh. Surely that should show us that there is no one beyond God's mercy.

One footnote to this account of Manasseh. Evil for most of his life, it is true that he repented near the end, forgiven by God and restored to his kingdom. However, when he died, his son, Amon, reigned in his place and followed his former example rather than his later one. Manasseh made his life right with God before his death but he had already corrupted his son so that Amon did not turn to the Lord, just because his father did. There is an important lesson in that for parents. Don't wait until your children are grown up to give your life to God. It may well be too late for them.

- Saul of Tarsus (Acts 8 and 9)

Convinced that Jesus was not the true Messiah, Saul did all he could to stamp out the influence of this carpenter's son from Nazareth. He made havoc of the church and tried to imprison and kill disciples of Christ. He did so with a totally clear conscience (Acts 23:1). But when he was convinced of his error, he turned to the Lord, accepted his gracious offer of forgiveness and became just as zealous for Christ as he had been against him, if not more so.

We Must Forgive Others

Now let's notice another series of verses. In these passages, we are told as Christians that we must be willing to forgive others. Before you consider these verses, let me point out two important things. First, it is clear that we cannot hope to be forgiven by the Lord if we are unwilling to be forgiving of others. Second, we are reminded often of our own forgiveness by God and that, if he could pardon us, surely we can give each other a break.

- Matthew 6:14-15—"For if you forgive men when they sin against you, your heavenly Father will also forgive you. But if you do not forgive men their sins, your Father will not forgive your sins."

- Mark 11:25-26—"Therefore I tell you, whatever you ask for in prayer, believe that you have received it, and it will be yours. And when you stand praying, if you hold anything against anyone, forgive him, so that your Father in heaven may forgive you your sins."

- Luke 17:1-5—"Jesus said to his disciples, 'Things that cause people to sin are bound to come, but woe to that person through whom they come. It would be better for him to be thrown into the sea with a millstone tied around his neck than for him to cause one of these little ones to sin. So watch yourselves. If your brother sins, rebuke him, and if he repents, forgive him. If he sins against you seven times in a day, and seven times comes back to you and says, "I repent," forgive him.' The apostles said to the Lord, 'Increase our faith!'"

- Colossians 3:13—"Bear with each other and forgive whatever grievances you may have against one another. Forgive as the Lord forgave you."

This is not an optional thing. We do not have a choice about whether we should forgive another or not. We must forgive others or we will be lost eternally. It's just that simple.

Two Important Passages

There are two passages that teach us some important principles about our dealings with others and our need to work out problems with finality.

- Matthew 18:15-17—"If your brother sins against you, go and show him his fault, just between the two of you. If he listens to you, you have won your brother over. But if he will not listen, take one or two others along, so that 'every matter may be established by the testimony of two or three witnesses.' If he refuses to listen to them, tell it to the church; and if he refuses to listen even to the church, treat him as you would a pagan or a tax collector."

The principle here is that if someone has sinned against you, *you* go to that person.

> • Matthew 5:23-24—"Therefore, if you are offering your gift at the altar and there remember that your brother has something against you, leave your gift there in front of the altar. First go and be reconciled to your brother; then come and offer your gift."

The principle in this verse is that if someone else thinks you have sinned, *you* go to that person.

If everyone would do that, you would meet each other in the middle. But, even if the other person is unwilling to meet you halfway, both passages (from the red letter teaching of Christ himself, I might add) tell you to take the first step by going to the person with whom you have differences.

It may well be true that some people do not deserve to be forgiven. But then, neither did we, but God forgave us anyway. He made salvation possible through the sacrifice of his Son on the cross. "Blessed are the merciful, for they will be shown mercy" (Matthew 5:7).

Conclusion

I don't know who said it originally, but I've heard several preachers repeat it and I like it. "Forgiveness and bitterness are the choices. Forgiveness feels better." Isn't that great? Isn't that true?

Let me close with two of my favorite verses in one of my favorite books of the New Testament. "Get rid of all bitterness, rage and anger, brawling and slander, along with every form of malice. Be kind and compassionate to one another, forgiving each other, just as in Christ God forgave you" (Ephesians 4:31-32). That's what the Bible teaches. Now the ball is in your court.

CHAPTER 8

Be Hospitable
to One Another

"Offer hospitality to one another without grumbling."
(1 Peter 4:9)

Hospitality is one of those things that has become a "lost art" over the last quarter of a century or so in America. Why is that? We have more money than ever, it is easier to get around from place to place, and we have many time-saving devices like microwaves, cell phones and computers. But there seems to be less hospitality than ever before.

That's an overstatement, of course. There are still those, and there always will be, who are extremely generous in their entertainment and friendship toward others.

But, for many of us, hospitality is a relic of the past. That's a shame and I want to write some things that I hope will reverse that trend, at least among the people of God.

A Commandment from God

We need to understand from the start that hospitality is a commandment of the Lord. This is another of those things that, for some unknown reason, some Christians have decided does not apply to them. It applies to others, but not to them.

How can one draw that conclusion? What passage of Scripture or principle from the Bible would even imply that hospitality is something we can choose not to do? Notice these verses:

> "Share with God's people who are in need. Practice hospitality" (Romans 12:13).

> "Keep on loving each other as brothers. Do not forget to entertain strangers, for by so doing some people have entertained angels without knowing it" (Hebrews 13:1-2).

> "Offer hospitality to one another without grumbling" (1 Peter 4:9).

Along with others, these passages clearly teach us that hospitality is a duty of Christians toward one another. This ought to be something we enjoy, an activity we look forward to with eager anticipation. Hospitality should be a highlight of our lives, not looked upon as some dreaded, legalistic duty. There should be no one we would rather spend time with than our brothers and sisters in Christ. Having others into our home is not the only way to do that, but it is a good way.

Some Bible Examples

There are some excellent examples of the ancient practice of hospitality in both testaments of the Bible. We need to learn some positive lessons from these people of faith who wanted to spend time with other people of God, sometimes at great personal expense and sacrifice. Let's notice a few cases of hospitality from each of the covenants.

• Abraham

> "The LORD appeared to Abraham near the great trees of Mamre while he was sitting at the entrance to his tent in the heat of the day. Abraham looked up and saw three men standing nearby. When he saw them, he hurried from the entrance of his tent to meet them and bowed low to the ground. He said, 'If I have found favor in your eyes, my lord, do not pass your servant by. Let a little water be brought, and then you may wash your feet and rest under this tree. Let me get you something to eat, so you can be refreshed and then go on your way—now that you have come to your servant.' 'Very

well,' they answered, 'do as you say.' So Abraham hurried into the tent to Sarah, 'Quick,' he said, 'get three seahs of fine flour and knead it and bake some bread.' Then he ran to the herd and selected a choice, tender calf and gave it to a servant, who hurried to prepare it. He then brought some curds and milk and the calf that had been prepared, and set these before them. While they ate, he stood near them under a tree" (Genesis 18:1-8).

Notice the three primary things Abraham did. First, he provided water for them to use in cleaning up, washing their feet and faces, etc. Then he gave them a place to rest under a comfortable tree. Thirdly, he gave them both food and drink to strengthen their bodies. Each of those three things would be a gesture that would provide refreshment and relief for those who were weary: a way to clean up, a place to rest, and nourishment. Those are the simple necessities of life and Abraham provided them for his guests.

And he didn't even know who they were. We know, of course, that they were angels, but he didn't know. One of them may well have been the Lord himself and some Bible students believe that this third individual (the other two were clearly angels) may have been an Old Testament appearance of Jesus. Whether this one was our Lord or not, they were messengers from God who had some important news for Abraham about the birth of Isaac and the imminent destruction of Sodom and Gomorrah. If Abraham had not been hospitable to them, who knows how these crucial events in God's plan might have played out differently.

• The Widow at Zarephath

"Some time later the brook dried up because there had been no rain in the land. Then the word of the LORD came to him (Elijah, rh): 'Go at once to Zarephath of Sidon and stay there. I have commanded a widow in that place to supply you with food.' So he went to Zarephath. When he came to the town gate, a widow was there gathering sticks. He called to her and asked, 'Would you bring me a little water in a jar so I may have a drink?' As she was going to get it, he called, 'And bring me, please, a piece of bread.' 'As surely as the

LORD your God lives,' she replied, 'I don't have any bread—only a handful of flour in a jar and a little oil in a jug. I am gathering a few sticks to take home and make a meal for myself and my son, that we may eat it—and die.' Elijah said to her, 'Don't be afraid. Go home and do as you have said. But first make a small cake of bread for me from what you have and bring it to me, and then make something for yourself and your son. For this is what the LORD, the God of Israel, says, "The jar of flour will not be used up and the jug of oil will not run dry until the day the LORD gives rain on the land."' She went away and did as Elijah had told her. So there was food every day for Elijah and for the woman and her family. For the jar of flour was not used up and the jug of oil did not run dry, in keeping with the word of the LORD spoken by Elijah" (1 Kings 17:7-16).

What a special opportunity to serve God this widow was given because of her generous spirit and hospitable nature. That's probably why the Lord used her to help Elijah in this time of great need—because that's the kind of servant she already was. (God usually uses people to serve him in great ways who are already serving him in small ways. He takes someone who is generous and big-hearted and uses them to help others. He doesn't take someone who is stingy and selfish and uninterested in others and magically or miraculously turn them into magnanimous, helpful, giving people.) Elijah was at a low point emotionally in his service to God and needed a boost. This widow and her son fed him food when it was needed.

• The Shunammite Woman

"One day Elisha went to Shunem. And a well-to-do woman was there, who urged him to stay for a meal. So whenever he came by, he stopped there to eat. She said to her husband, 'I know that this man who often comes our way is a holy man of God. Let's make a small room on the roof and put in it a bed and a table, a chair and a lamp for him. Then he can stay there whenever he comes to us'" (2 Kings 4:8-11).

It is especially interesting to me in this account that this hospitality had been going on for quite some time before the woman realizes that

Elisha is a holy man of God. Before that, she was simply showing kindness to a passing stranger. He needed food; she was well-to-do and able to provide for him and she took the initiative to help him. Later, as she figures out that Elisha is someone who is important, she takes the next step and suggests to her husband that they provide a regular place for Elisha to stay. They invest the time and money to build a guest room onto their home and make it as comfortable as possible for Elisha when he stays there. It was out of the kindness and generosity of her heart that she helps Elisha by being hospitable to him.

There is an interesting addendum to this story, found as the chapter continues (2 Kings 4:11-37). Some years later, after the woman and her husband have a child, the boy and his father are working out in the field and the boy suffers some serious head injury, perhaps a stroke, an aneurysm, a brain tumor or something similar. The child dies. Immediately, the woman searches for Elisha who returns home with her and miraculously brings the boy back to life again. Maybe he would have done so anyway. But, you can't help but wonder if this miracle wasn't the woman's reward for her kind hospitality to the holy man, Elisha.

• The Early Christians

In Acts 2 and Acts 4, we are told that the first century Christians took care of each other's physical needs. They shared material things with one another and made certain that no one was overlooked. They spent much time together in each other's homes and some of them even sold possessions to meet the needs of their brothers and sisters in Christ. What an excellent example for us of how we ought to help each other, as the need arises. But, we should not wait for a crisis to arise before we do that. We ought to be meeting each other's needs on a regular basis; it should be an every day occurrence that Christians spend time together in a social and recreational setting, practicing hospitality and serving one another.

• Lydia

"One of those listening was a woman named Lydia, a dealer in purple cloth from the city of Thyatira, who was a worshiper of God.

The Lord opened her heart to respond to Paul's message. When she and the members of her household were baptized, she invited us into her home. 'If you consider me a believer in the Lord,' she said, 'come and stay at my house.' And she persuaded us" (Acts 16:14-15).

Lydia was a successful and, no doubt, busy business woman. She was from Thyatira, lived in Philippi and conducted business in purple cloth (the color of royalty and wealth). But, she was interested in spiritual things and, when she went to the riverside with other women and heard the gospel message being presented by Paul and Silas, she became a Christian. Not content to stop there in her obedience to the Lord, she invited Paul and Silas (Luke was there also; notice the word "us." There may have been others also.) into her home to stay. The New King James Version says that she "constrained" them. She simply would not take no for an answer. In spite of the expense and the time required to provide for their needs, she knew this was a way she could encourage those who were taking the gospel to the uttermost parts of the earth. Like so many, she wanted to help and hospitality was one of the areas where she could do so.

• Onesiphorus

"May the Lord show mercy to the household of Onesiphorus, because he often refreshed me and was not ashamed of my chains. On the contrary, when he was in Rome, he searched hard for me until he found me. May the Lord grant that he will find mercy from the Lord on that day! You know very well in how many ways he helped me in Ephesus" (2 Timothy 1:16-18).

Onesiphorus (aren't you glad our names are simpler than some of those in Bible times?) was a friend of Paul's. The apostle says, "he often refreshed me." In other words, helping Paul was one of his passions. He helped Paul, according to this passage, both in Rome, where he served Paul while the latter was in prison, and in his hometown of Ephesus, where Timothy was serving the church at the time of this letter. Second Timothy was Paul's last letter and he knew his death was nearing. One of the things that kept him going was the memory of so many who had been good to him. (There were also some who had mistreated him.)

But he wanted good people like Timothy, Onesiphorus, Lois, Eunice, Crescens, Titus, Luke, Mark, Tychicus, Carpus, Priscilla and Aquila, Erastus, Trophimus and others to get what they deserved also. And what they deserved was blessing and mercy from God. They had all helped Paul in various ways and he was deeply grateful for their love and service. They received the honor of being mentioned in the word of God in a positive way and, of course, it is implied that they will receive an eternal reward from the Lord, as well.

Who Needs Hospitality?

There are several people the Bible indicates ought to be the recipients of our hospitality. It can be summarized by saying that we should be hospitable to those we know and to those we don't know. I guess that about covers it. Let's look at each of these briefly.

We should spend a significant amount of time with people we know. Read again Acts 2:44-47. The first century disciples obviously spent much time together, both in public worship settings and in homes. We need to follow their example and work hard to develop close friendships with each other. We should pray together and play together. We should go on picnics together, eat together (most Christians like to do that), play games together, maybe even travel together. We should evangelize in groups (maybe having someone else with us would take away some of the fear factor). We should go to good, clean movies together, visit the shut-ins and nursing homes together and did I mention that we should eat together? The Christians we worship with ought to be our dearest friends.

But we also need to spend time with some people we don't know very well. As a matter of fact, the word hospitality literally means, "love of strangers." We should reach out beyond our own comfort zone and be eager to embrace people who are not our close acquaintances.

If the church where you worship has much size at all, there are probably people in the congregation you don't know well. The so-called experts tell us that, in any group, you can only be intimately familiar with about forty people, at the most. After that, the group automatically sub-divides into smaller groups. That's why so many churches have started small group arrangements of one kind or another to meet the needs of the people within those natural divisions. Look around you at the next service. Intentionally seek out someone you don't know very well and make a special point to meet them. Most people are pretty shy, by nature, and therefore, if you don't initiate the effort to introduce yourself and get to know them, it probably won't happen. We all need to work harder to do this. We are a family and we need to make certain that everyone feels at home.

There are always going to be those who feel disenfranchised by the church. In other words, they feel like outsiders, rather than a real part of what is going on. And most people don't like being outsiders. Hospitality is one of the best ways we can reach out to those who need to be loved and show them that we care about them and want to help them and spend time with them getting to know them.

We also should meet visitors to our services. You never know if a visitor is a Christian or trying to find the Lord. How we treat them may well determine their eternal destiny. If we are warm and affirming of them, they may study, learn more about God and become Christians. If we don't welcome them, they may never come back again. I have heard that Ghandi was investigating Christianity at one point in his life, but when he visited a "Christian church," he was treated so poorly that he left convinced that there was no truth to Christianity. I don't know the veracity of the story, but whether it happened to Ghandi or not, it has happened to lots of other people. And that's a shame. Let's make it a point to repent and do better.

One More Thing

Don't worry about having to make it fancy. One of the reasons more people don't practice more hospitality is that they think they have to really do it up fancy or it's not worth it. I believe that's a mistake. Some of the greatest times I have enjoyed with others was sitting around a campfire, cooking hot dogs, roasting marshmallows, talking about spiritual things and singing "psalms, hymns and spiritual songs" from memory. It didn't cost anybody much of anything and they didn't even have to clean up their house.

Two families might put their leftovers together and each eat what the other one brought. (It wasn't a rerun for them!) Two families might pitch in together and take a third couple out to eat at a fast food restaurant. The possibilities are unlimited if we aren't trying to impress each other, but simply desiring to spend some time together building each other up in our mutual work in the kingdom. Be creative. Work out your own specifics. But do something to be hospitable to others.

Some Practical Examples of Hospitality

- having a party at your house so teens will have some wholesome entertainment.
- inviting visitors to your home for a snack after services.
- hosting the evangelist or teacher in your home during a revival or special series of meetings.
- having a weiner roast in your back yard.
- sharing a sandwich or a bowl of soup with a friend who stops in at mealtime.
- opening your home to friends who are just passing through town.
- making your home available for a night of gospel singing.
- having out-of-town Christians who visit services on Sunday into your home for lunch.
- inviting Christians and non-Christians over to your house or apartment for a Bible study.
- being friendly to all who come your way.
- hosting some people for a meal in your home who could never return the favor (Luke 14:12-14).
- doing "good to all people, especially to those who belong to the family of believers" (Galatians 6:10).

No Hospitality for These

There are certain people that the Bible tells us we ought not to entertain in any social way.

- The immoral and ungodly believer

  "I have written you in my letter not to associate with sexually immoral people—not at all meaning the people of this world who are immoral, or the greedy and swindlers, or idolaters. In that case you would have to leave this world. But now I am writing you that you must not associate with anyone who calls himself a brother but is sexually immoral or greedy, an idolater or a slanderer, a drunkard or a swindler. With such a man do not even eat" (1 Corinthians 5:9-11).

  It seems a shame, in some ways, that this passage is even in the Bible. There should be no such thing as a Christian who involves himself in these ungodly activities and refuses to repent. But the reality is that even disciples of the Lord can get caught up in sin and, when that happens, the Lord tells us not to associate with them, in the hope that they will realize their error and return to him. In the first century, eating a meal with another often symbolized acceptance and approval of that one. That's why the Jews wouldn't eat with Gentiles and why the scribes and Pharisees criticized Jesus for eating with tax collectors and sinners. The Bible is teaching us not to do anything that would seem to lend our approval to a sinful lifestyle that one will not change. Show no hospitality for this one.

- The lazy

  "For even when we were with you, we gave you this rule: 'If a man will not work, he shall not eat'" (2 Thessalonians 3:10).

  That one is pretty self-explanatory. One who "will not work" must not be the recipient of our hospitality. He is not talking about those who cannot work due to health related issues. He is not speaking of those who have been laid off from their work, have looked diligently for something to do, but simply hasn't found the right position. He is speaking of those who are capable of working and choose not to do so.

- False teachers

  "Anyone who runs ahead and does not continue in the teaching of Christ does not have God; whoever continues in the teaching has both the Father and the Son. If anyone comes to you and does not bring this teaching, do not take him into your house or welcome him. Anyone who welcomes him shares in his wicked work" (2 John 9-11).

Those who perpetuate religious error that will damn the souls of those who believe and accept their heresy must not be encouraged in any way. He tells us not to take such a one into our home, not to welcome him, not to help him (the old King James says, "bid him godspeed") at all in his work of spreading false doctrine. We need to compare what a person teaches with the word of God (see Acts 17:11 and 1 John 4:1) and reject those who teach anything contrary to the Bible. Do not show hospitality to one who is truly an anti-Christ.

Conclusion

Hospitality is one of the greatest blessings of the Christian life, whether given or received. The time we get to spend together with fellow believers is invaluable in strengthening our souls to live faithfully. It is a win-win situation for everybody. You win, the other person wins, and the Lord wins. Let's not allow good, old-fashioned hospitality to die out in our lifetime, as long as we have the opportunity to serve others in this way.

CHAPTER 9

Do Not Speak Against One Another

"Do not speak evil of one another, brethren. He who speaks evil
of his brother, speaks evil of the law and judges the law. But if you
judge the law, you are not a doer of the law but a judge."
(James 4:11, NKJV)

This is the only chapter we will study in the negative. With all of the others, we have discussed things we should do for each other. In this chapter, we focus on something we are not to do, namely speaking evil of one another.

It is vitally important that we speak properly to each other. Words have tremendous power to build up or to destroy. As we seek to help one another grow into the image of Christ, we must use caution not to destroy the Lord's work with our mouths. Too often, we speak without thinking about the consequences. There are many verses and numerous principles that deal with this subject and we must heed those warnings.

Sins of the Tongue

There are many sins that we can commit with the tongue. Our mouths can get us into trouble quickly and it may take a long time to undo the damage that we can cause because we did not restrain ourselves when we should have. Once said, words can't be taken back and, therefore, we must be very careful about what we say to others.

Grumbling

"And do not grumble, as some of them (the ancient Israelites in the wilderness) did—and were killed by the destroying angel" (1 Corinthians 10:10). In context, Paul is warning the Christians in Corinth to avoid those sins that caused the Lord to be displeased with his people in the Old Testament. Notice verses 5 and 6—"Nevertheless, God was not pleased with most of them; their bodies were scattered over the desert. Now these things occurred as examples to keep us from setting our hearts on evil things as they did." He then gives a number of specific sins that the Lord's people must flee. He mentions lusting after evil things (verse 6), idolatry (verse 7), sexual immorality (verse 8), testing the Lord (verse 9) and grumbling (verse 10).

One of the easiest things in the world to do is to criticize and find fault with those who are trying to do something good. Rather than jump in with both feet to help, some want to sit around and take pot shots at those who are working in the kingdom. Such murmuring causes a constant undercurrent of doubt, suspicion and distrust. It undermines the peace that ought to exist in a congregation, causes the formation of "cliques," affects others as we seek to bring them over to "our side," and results in a bunch of small groups within the church, all thinking they have all the answers. It does nothing to build up the church; such attitudes only destroy. Grumbling takes no intelligence at all, is a sign of spiritual immaturity and shows no concern for the spiritual well being of others.

God had some rather strong words to say about grumblers. "See, the Lord is coming with thousands upon thousands of his holy ones to judge everyone, and to convict all the ungodly of all the ungodly acts they have done in the ungodly way, and of all the harsh words ungodly sinners have spoken against him.

These men are grumblers and faultfinders; they follow their own evil desires; they boast about themselves and flatter others for their own advantage" (Jude 14b-16). Jude makes five points about grumblers.

1. They are following their own evil desires. They are not concerned with serving and pleasing God, but themselves.

2. They boast about themselves. The New King James Version says that they "mouth great swelling words." Have you ever known anyone who complained about himself? Faultfinders think they are always right and everyone else is wrong. They need to look in the mirror.

3. They flatter others to gain personal advantage. Flattery is not a sincere compliment. It is an attempt to "smooth talk" others so they will do something we want them to do. Such partiality is shown because of the things others can do for us. This is often more important than the truth.

4. Grumblers are ungodly. Doesn't that just stand out in the above passage? He uses the word "ungodly" four times to speak of their actions, thoughts, consequences and words. Everything about such people is ungodly and wicked.

5. The final result is that they will be lost. When the Lord comes in judgment, grumblers will be punished for their unrighteous talk.

There are several other words that could be used to describe this same sin. Griping, whining, complaining, pouting, criticizing, and murmuring are all synonyms for the sin of grumbling. It really doesn't matter what you call it. God hates it. Let's be sure we aren't guilty of this sin!

Lying

We look with disgust on the sins of fornication, drunkenness, robbery and murder, and rightly so, for they are abominable to the Lord. But some look lightly on the sin of lying and rationalize that "everyone does it," so it must not be too big a deal. However, this sin is listed as one of the seven things that the Lord hates (Proverbs 6:16-19).

Lying is another of the easiest sins to commit with the tongue and is, therefore, one of the most common sins in the world. All too often, we have done something we shouldn't have done and when someone confronts us about it, the first impulse is often to make something up that will make us look better. We might lie to cover up our mistakes (politicians have made an art form of this). We might make up a story in an attempt to bail ourselves out in a time of trouble. Rather than to face the consequences of our actions, it is sometimes easier to fabricate an alternative course.

There are numerous verses that condemn this sin. A couple should suffice to make the point. "Therefore each of you must put off falsehood and speak truthfully to his neighbor, for we are all members of one body" (Ephesians 4:25). This verse speaks directly to the point that we are making here. He tells us to put off lying and put on truthfulness, because of our mutual membership in the body of Christ. Members of the same body must not lie to one another.

"Do not lie to each other, since you have taken off your old self with its practices and have put on the new self, which is being renewed in knowledge in the image of its Creator" (Colossians 3:9-10). Here, the apostle equates lying with the former person we used to be before Christ came into our lives and makes it clear that such behavior is not to be a part of what we are now. Even those who used to have a big problem telling the truth must make certain that they are now truthful in all of their speech.

Lying is from Satan. Jesus said this to some ungodly people who were attacking him. "You belong to your father, the devil, and you want to carry out your father's desire. He was a murderer from the beginning, not holding to the truth, for there is no truth in him. When he lies, he speaks his own native language, for he is a liar and the father of lies" (John 8:44). Satan does not hold to the truth, there is no truth in him, lies are his own native language and he is the father of all lies. That's pretty strong language, but certainly true. The most frightening part of it all, however, is that the Lord was telling his audience that they belonged to the devil because of the lying and deceitfulness of their own lives. Could that be true of us, as well? It is a strong warning to us, at the very least, to be very careful about how we handle the truth. It is never right to lie, no matter what the circumstances might be. Honesty really is the best policy, because it is God's policy. "For we are taking pains to do what is right, not only in the eyes of the Lord but also in the eyes of men" (2 Corinthians 8:21).

Slander

Slander refers to making a false accusation against another. At times, it is simply translated as "evil speaking" about another person. Interestingly enough, it comes from the Greek word, *diabolos*, from which we get our English word, diabolical, and from which the word, devil, is derived. Satan is described in Revelation 12:10 as "the accuser of our brothers." One of his favorite tactics is to cause people to look down on Christians.

Well, that might be understandable of Satan, but why in the world would one Christian slander another disciple? The love that we are to have for one another should make us never want to do that to someone else (isn't that what the Golden Rule says?).

Slander is found in the list of sins in 2 Corinthians 12:20. It was one of the things that Paul wanted the Corinthians to purge from their midst before he arrived there for a visit. He said, "For I am afraid that when I come I may not find you as I want you to be, and you may not find me as you want me to be. I fear that there may be quarreling, jealousy, outbursts of anger, factions, slander, gossip, arrogance and disorder." Slander is listed along with some other unsavory characteristics, isn't it? Surely no faithful disciple of the Lord would want to be guilty of that. Ephesians 4:31 lists slander as one of the things that a Christian must "get rid of."

Gossip

Gossip can be a major source of strife in a local church. It is very powerful stuff. Gossip can divide a church, break up a home, ruin a reputation, shatter someone's happiness and destroy someone's life.

Several of the Proverbs deal with this grievous sin. Notice just a few of them.

"A gossip betrays a confidence, but a trustworthy man keeps a secret" (11:13).

"A perverse man stirs up dissension, and a gossip separates close friends" (16:28).

"A gossip betrays a confidence, so avoid a man who talks too much" (20:19).

"Without wood a fire goes out; without gossip a quarrel dies down" (26:20).

There are, again, several biblical terms for those who gossip, like whisperers, talebearers, backbiters, and busybodies.

Here are four questions we should always ask ourselves before repeating something about others.

1. Is it true? If it isn't, then we should not even consider telling it.

2. Even if it is true, will it do any good to tell it? Just because something is true, doesn't mean that it would be wise to tell others about it.

3. Is it necessary? Or is it just something "juicy" that I can't wait to tell?

4. Would I say it in the presence of that person? If I wouldn't say it around that individual, then I shouldn't say it behind his back either.

Profanity

"Do not let any unwholesome talk come out of your mouth, but only what is helpful for building others up according to their needs, that it may benefit those who listen" (Ephesians 4:29). Unwholesome talk could include any number of things. The New King James renders that phrase as "corrupt communication." The idea, clearly, is that some things we can say are ungodly, that they tear others down spiritually, rather than building them up or strengthening them. Using bad language, telling dirty jokes, taking the Lord's name in vain are all examples of that kind of unwholesome communication.

In the next chapter of Ephesians, Paul said this (5:3-4), "But among you there must not be even a hint of sexual immorality, or of any kind of impurity, or of greed, because these are improper for God's holy people. Nor should there be obscenity, foolish talk or coarse joking, which are out of place, but rather thanksgiving." Those verses describe exactly what Paul had in mind. Sexually immoral things, impure things, obscenities, coarse jokes are all "improper for God's holy people." There ought not even to be a hint of those things among the people of the Lord.

Angry words

Briefly, I also want to mention that we must control our anger as it applies to the tone of speaking we do around one another. It is easy to say words in anger that we really don't mean, but once we say them, they can't be taken back. James warns us of this problem in James 1:19-20. "My dear brothers, take note of this: Everyone should be quick to listen, slow to speak and slow to become angry, for man's anger does not bring about the righteous life that God desires." Someone has pointed out that God made us with two ears and only one mouth, so that, on average, we should listen as least twice as much as we speak. That's not a bad rule to follow. Rarely does one regret his silence, but many have regretted things they have said.

While driving down the street recently, I saw a church sign that said, "Think twice; speak once." That's a really admirable motto to follow.

Good Uses of the Tongue

However, this discussion should not be one-sided. While it is true that there are many warnings about misusing the tongue, we must also realize the power of our words to do good. There are many godly, appropriate, righteous ways we should use our tongues. Here are just a few of them.

Teaching the truth

"You must teach what is in accord with sound doctrine" (Titus 2:1). There will always be plenty of false teachers around (Titus 1:10-16) so people are needed who will use their abilities to teach truth. This would include the evangelizing of the lost (Mark 1:17) and the building up of the saved (Ephesians 4:15-16).

Helping others to correct sin

"Brothers, if someone is caught in a sin, you who are spiritual should restore him gently. But watch yourself, or you also may be tempted" (Galatians 6:1). This is not easy to do, but it is important work for the Lord. Those who are drifting away, or who have completely quit trying, need to be encouraged to do what is right. Think about it; if you were losing your faith, wouldn't you want someone to care enough to try to help you?

Strengthening and encouraging others

"Do not let any unwholesome talk come out of your mouths, but only what is helpful for building others up according to their needs, that it may benefit those who listen" (Ephesians 4:29). Sometimes people just need to hear an encouraging word. They need to know that others care about them and are concerned about their spiritual welfare. Barnabas was called "the Son of Encouragement" by the apostles (Acts 4:36; see chapter 4). Let's build each other up, not tear each other down.

Praising God

"Through Jesus, therefore, let us continually offer to God a sacrifice of praise—the fruit of lips that confess his name" (Hebrews 13:15). True worship helps draw us closer to God and to one another, but primarily worship is for the purpose of glorifying the name of the Lord.

Expressing gratitude

"Every good and perfect gift is from above, coming down from the Father of the heavenly lights, who does not change like shifting shadows" (James 1:17). We must be grateful to God for all the wonderful blessings we enjoy in life. And we should not be ashamed to thank God, even around others for those gifts.

Prayer

"Pray continually" (1 Thessalonians 5:17). The New King James Version says, "Pray without ceasing." Prayer is our ability to communicate the feelings of our heart to our heavenly Father. It ought not to be a burden or simply a responsibility, but a divine privilege. Pray often and sincerely (James 5:16).

Humor

"A cheerful heart is good medicine, but a crushed spirit dries up the bones" (Proverbs 17:22). This is not referring to dirty, vulgar jokes or to ridiculing and making fun of others, which is the idea many have of humor these days. This is good, clean, non-hurtful humor. It makes the day go better and can be a real blessing to our lives. Sometimes we just need to lighten up. "The tongue that brings healing (a wholesome tongue, NKJV) is a tree of life, but a deceitful tongue crushes the spirit" (Proverbs 15:4).

One Additional Thought

It is bad enough that we sometimes speak against one another to one another. But it is very foolish and damaging to the cause of Christ when we speak against other Christians to unbelievers. Some of the problems we have in trying to convert people lies in the fact that their opinion of the church is already poor and sometimes that has happened because of things that Christians have said about their fellow disciples. We must exercise extreme caution not to criticize the church in front of non-Christians or even for believers for that matter. This applies to our own children, as well. Don't cause them to grow up with a negative feeling about God because of criticism you have leveled at the church.

Conclusion

Jesus taught in Matthew 12:37, "For by your words you will be acquitted, and by your words you will be condemned." One of the standards of judgment that the Judge will use in the last day, one that will determine whether some people spend eternity in heaven or in hell, will be how they have used their mouths. If you will be saved or lost based on your tongue, what will your fate be? This is a more serious issue than many Christians realize (see James 1:26). I hope this discussion of the subject will help you.

CHAPTER 10

Accept One Another

"May the God who gives endurance and encouragement give you a spirit of unity among yourselves as you follow Christ Jesus, so that with one heart and mouth you may glorify the God and Father of our Lord Jesus Christ. Accept one another, then, just as Christ has accepted you, in order to bring praise to God."
(Romans 15:5-7)

When it comes to relationships in the church, everyone is to be included. There should not be any insiders and outsiders, or haves and have-nots in the church. We are all one in Christ Jesus. That's one of the unique qualities of Christianity that distinguishes it from other world religions. Everyone is equal in the eyes of the Lord.

Church growth material generally refers to the process of welcoming new members as "assimilation." One of the primary differences between growing churches and those that are shrinking is how they treat new members. Most churches can bring people in the front door. Growing churches have learned some secrets about how to close the back door. There are three keys to understanding how to assimilate new people into the fellowship of a local church and each of these is related to a "one another" command. Those keys are learning to accept one another, considering one another, and being devoted to each other. This chapter will take a brief look at each of these responsibilities.

Accept One Another

As the above passage from Romans 15 teaches, we are to accept others as our spiritual equals, even if they are different from us in some way. The New King James Version translates that phrase as "Receive one another" and, again, carries the idea of including everyone in the Lord's work.

When Jesus Christ died on the cross for the sins of the world, he did so for everybody. He did not die for only a select few, although there will be many who reject God's gracious offer of salvation. "But we see Jesus, who was made a little lower than the angels, now crowned with glory and honor because he suffered death, so that by the grace of God he might taste death for everyone" (Hebrews 2:9). Paul said the same thing, in Titus 2:11, "For the grace of God that brings salvation has appeared to all men." God's grace is for everyone, not just a few.

One of the first principles of God's dealing with mankind is that he shows no partiality or favoritism. The (Old) King James said that God is "no respecter of persons." God created every person who has ever lived and, if he made them, with their own distinctive qualities, he is not going to hold those qualities against them. People who are white are white because God made them white. People who are black are black because God made them black. The same thing is true of those who are brown, yellow, red or any other skin tone. He also made people short or tall, blue eyed or green eyed, Jew or Gentile. God loves everybody, just as they are.

Peter said, as he preached at the household of Cornelius, the first Gentile converts to Christ, "I now realize how true it is that God does not show favoritism but accepts men from every nation who fear him and do what is right" (Acts 10:34-35). Paul stated, as he was pointing out the common sinful condition of both Jew and Gentile, "For God does not show favoritism" (Romans 2:11). God does not see people differently; he looks at us all alike.

If we are God's children, we must treat others as he does. If we show partiality or respect of persons, we are guilty before God of grievous sin. "But if you show favoritism, you sin and are convicted by the law as lawbreakers" (James 2:9). Prejudice (our modern term for "respect of persons") is despicable and we must make every effort to avoid this travesty.

As our Master was dying on the cross, one of the things he said was "It is finished" (John 19:30). While there are many possible things he could have been referring to, one of those things was clearly the distinction between people that had long existed in the world.

Peter's vision (Acts 10:9-16) not only released eating restrictions of the law on certain foods, it also ended all distinctions between people. The most obvious one is the wall between Jew and Gentile that was so prevalent in the first century. The animosity that had developed over the centuries was deep- rooted in years of aggression and hostility. It was far more than a religious difference in interpretation of a few passages from the Old Testament. It was societal, religious, cultural, and many other things. It is difficult for those of us who are so far removed from it to appreciate the depth of the hatred each felt for the other. The closest comparison for us Americans would be the hostilities between blacks and whites that have been dominant in our culture for years. As unjust as many of those feelings have been and with all the cruelties that have taken place over the years, even that does not approach the animosity between Jew and Gentile.

Paul describes the alienation of the Gentiles from the Lord in Ephesians 2. "Therefore, remember that formerly you who are Gentiles by birth and called 'uncircumcised' by those who call themselves 'the circumcision' (that done in the body by the hands of men)—remember that at that time you were separate from Christ, excluded from citizenship in Israel and foreigners to the covenants of the promise, without hope and without God in the world. But now in Christ Jesus you who once were far away have been brought near through the blood of Christ. For he himself is our peace, who has made the two one and has destroyed the barrier, the dividing wall of hostility, by abolishing in his flesh the law with its commandments and regulations. His purpose was to create in himself one new man out of the two, thus making peace, and in this one body to reconcile both of them to God through the cross, by which he put to death their hostility. He came and preached peace to you who were far away and peace to those who were near. For through him we both have access to the Father by one Spirit" (verses 11-18).

Notice that this passage uses words to describe the before/after condition of the Gentiles, words like separate, excluded, foreigners, without hope, without God, far away, barrier, the dividing wall of hostility. And it teaches that, in Christ, everyone is now accepted by the Lord and at peace with him. There is no longer such a thing as Jew and Gentile. We can all have a close relationship to God.

Paul taught the same thing in Galatians 3:26-29. "You are all sons of God through faith in Christ Jesus, for all of you who were baptized into Christ have clothed yourselves with Christ. There is neither Jew nor Greek, slave nor free, male nor female, for you are all one in Christ Jesus. If you belong to Christ, then you are Abraham's seed, and heirs according to the promise."

Christ said, in the greatest of all commissions, that the gospel was to be preached to "every creature" (Mark 16:15, NKJV). Because all sin (Romans 3:23) and the punishment for sin is death (Romans 6:23), everyone needs the gospel, the good news of salvation. No culture, language, skin color, nation or group of people is to be excluded from fellowship with God. It doesn't matter if one is Jew or Gentile, slave or free, rich or poor, red or yellow, black or white, we are all one in Christ. All distinctions ended at the cross of Jesus Christ.

In Acts 6, when there was a legitimate problem between "Grecian Jews" and "Hebraic Jews" over the care of Grecian widows, the two groups got together with the apostles and solved the problem to everyone's satisfaction. There is no evidence that one group even considered splitting the church and starting their own church. There could easily have developed two congregations in Jerusalem, a Grecian church and a Hebraic church. That's how many people would handle the problem today. But, under the inspired leadership of the apostles, they simply resolved the problem and went on worshiping the Lord together. That's a New Testament pattern we must restore.

Returning to our text in Romans 15, the apostle tells the early disciples to receive one another, in spite of their differences. Chapter 14 is on the same subject and explains that as former Jews and former Gentiles, they had several disagreements over the observance of certain feast days and the eating of meats that had been sacrificed to idols. Some did those things and others were convinced that those things were wrong. In addition, the question of circumcision had divided many saints in various congregations (see Galatians 2). Paul's advice to them in view of the differences of opinion on these matters was that they just needed to accept each other as Christians. Such differences did not affect their fellowship with God and ought not to affect their relationship with each other. There are many such issues today that churches have split over that should never have caused a breaking of fellowship. Surely more harmony and peace could be maintained if people had a greater sense of responsibility to "accept one another."

Consider One Another

"Let us hold unswervingly to the hope we profess, for he who promised is faithful. And let us consider how we may spur one another on toward love and good deeds. Let us not give up meeting together, as some are in the habit of doing, but let us encourage one another—and all the more as you see the Day approaching" (Hebrews 10:23-25).

The writer of Hebrews was trying to help these Christians realize that they needed to remain true to the Lord. In this section of his letter, he gave them several commands that would result in greater faithfulness. There are five verbs (action words, as English teachers describe them) about our duties. Let's look at each of them.

1. **Hold unswervingly.**

   This, of course, means to not abandon. Christians should hold on firmly to their faith in Jesus Christ. At the time, many were turning back to Judaism, some to the world. He is showing them that they must not quit serving God. Even if others gave up, they must not. He added this admonition in verses 35-39. "So do not throw away your confidence; it will be richly rewarded. You need to persevere so that when you have done the will of God, you will receive what he has promised. For in just a very little while, 'He who is coming will come and will not delay. But my righteous one will live by faith. And if he shrinks back, I will not be pleased with him.' But we are not of those who shrink back and are destroyed, but of those who believe and are saved." The word "unswervingly" means without wavering, literally, without bending, being consistently faithful to what God had taught them. They should be faithful to God, even if no one else was.

2. Consider one another.

This speaks of thoughtfully looking to help each other, thinking about what we can do to help others remain faithful. Once we have committed ourselves to doing what is right, we must help others to make that same commitment. In connection with our need to meet regularly with other Christians, he says we should attend with the idea of "how can I help others to grow and mature?", not simply asking, "what do I get out of worship or Bible class?" Being considerate of others means we must look out for others, not just self. We think about how our words and actions affect others. We consciously seek for ideas about how we can edify our fellow disciples. Paul said it this way. "Therefore, as God's chosen people, holy and dearly loved, clothe yourselves with compassion, kindness, humility, gentleness and patience. Bear with each other and forgive whatever grievances you may have against one another. Forgive as the Lord forgave you. And over all these virtues put on love, which binds them all together in perfect unity" (Colossians 3:12-14). Considering others means putting them before your own needs and desires.

3. Spur one another on toward love and good deeds.

This refers to our need to challenge other people to be all they can be for God. Some versions say we are to "provoke" each other to love and good works. The idea is to stimulate or sharpen others so that they will be helped along the way to do more of the will of the Lord. A primary purpose for our assemblies is to remind us of our duties toward Him. A secondary purpose is to remind others of those responsibilities, as well. The writer of Proverbs said, "As iron sharpens iron, so one man sharpens another" (27:17). We need each other in the body of Christ, so we can help one another to grow beyond our comfort zone and to develop our abilities in the kingdom.

4. Let us not give up meeting together.

This is an encouragement to be faithful and regular in attendance at the services of the church. The New King James Version says, "Not forsaking the assembling of ourselves together." If Christians get into the habit of forsaking assemblies, they will eventually lose their faith. Some were not growing as they should (Hebrews 5:12) and perhaps this was the result of not attending regularly. You cannot grow spiritually if you refuse to be faithful in attendance and you cannot help others to grow either. Someone once said the only reason why someone should not attend Bible study is because they already know the whole Bible. But, if they really know the whole Bible, they need to be there to share their deep knowledge with others. So, in reality, there is no good reason to not attend. We do not live in a vacuum. We need others and they need us. That's why we all need the church. It is possible to study the Bible personally and grow spiritually, but do most people who are unfaithful in attendance with a local church have a strong, personal devotional life? Think about it.

5. Encourage one another.

This reminds us that we should use this assembly time to help each other. It is to be an encouraging time, characterized by warmth, friendliness and love. It should be a time when we are happy to be together as a family. Speak to others before and after services. Use this time to talk to others, especially those you don't know very well and those who don't get enough attention. Help single mothers with children and no husband there to help. Greet visitors to our assemblies. Don't get into little huddles with people you see all the time while ignoring others.

As we sing, we are to "speak to one another in psalms, hymns and spiritual songs" (Ephesians 5:19). The Lord's Supper is to be a time when we "commune" (that's why it's sometimes called communion) with God and each other. Even our prayers are to be joint prayers, led by one, but offered to God by all. The church has an important place in the plan of God for our growth and development.

As we "consider one another," it is important, again, to realize that some get left out of such considerations. No one is to be overlooked. I don't believe that Christians intentionally ignore others, but sometimes we get into routines and fail to think about the needs of other disciples.

This poem by an unknown author expresses well the need to think about the needs and situations of others. It is entitled, "If We Knew Each Other Better."

> If we knew each other better,
>   We would praise where we now blame,
>
> We would know each bears his burden,
>   Wears some hidden cross of shame.
>
> We would feel the heartaches bitter
>   They so long alone have borne.
>
> If we knew each other better,
>   We would praise instead of scorn.
>
> If we knew each other better,
>   You and I and all the rest,
>
> Seeing down beneath the surface
>   To the sorrows all unguessed,
>
> We would quit our cold complaining,
>   And a hand of trust extend,
>
> If we knew each other better,
>   We would count each one a friend.
>
> We can know each other better
>   If we take the time to try,
>
> Little deeds of loving kindness,
>   Make a better by and by.
>
> Just a look of understanding
>   Brings a touch of all mankind;
>
> We can know each other better
>   Yes, seeking, we shall find.

Be Devoted to One Another

"Be devoted to one another in brotherly love. Honor one another above yourselves" (Romans 12:10). To be devoted to someone means to be committed to that person's happiness and success. A person who is devoted to a job puts in long, hard, sacrificial hours while trying to please the boss. A person who is devoted to another Christian will work long and hard, making sacrifices when necessary to help others be more pleasing to God. The idea, as Paul expressed it, is to put others above self. "Do nothing out of selfish ambition or vain conceit, but in humility consider others better than yourselves. Each of you should look not only to your own interests, but also to the interests of others" (Philippians 2:3-4). It's just human nature to take care of ourselves, but we need to learn to take care of others also. If we will be devoted to others, as we accept them in Christ and as we consider their needs, we will all grow together into the image of Christ, who put the needs of lost humanity above his own, and died on the cross for the whole world.

As Christians, we are brothers and sisters in Christ. One of our spiritual blessings as those who are "in Christ" (Ephesians 1:3) is the devotion and love of the family of God. The church is not they, it is we. It is not them, it is us. It is not "those people," it is all of us who share what Peter called "a like precious faith" (NKJV). The church is our common bond. My Savior is your Savior. My Lord is your Lord. My heaven is your heaven. My God is your God. We share something special that no one else in the world can understand. We have "the peace of God that passes understanding" and have obeyed "the unsearchable riches of Christ." We are one in the Lord. We are to be devoted to each other.

Conclusion

Think about these words from the inspired pen of the beloved apostle, John. "This is the message we have heard from him and declare to you: God is light; in him there is no darkness at all. If we claim to have fellowship with him yet walk in darkness, we lie and do not live by the truth. But if we walk in the light, as he is in the light, we have fellowship with one another, and the blood of Jesus, his Son, purifies us from all sin" (1 John 1:5-7). As we live our daily lives for God, we must always remember the dimension of our faith that puts us in relationship with other Christians. As the Lord adds people to the church (Acts 2:47), that puts us into a relationship with all other saved people on the face of the whole earth. Many of them we will never meet until we reach heaven. But, on the local level, we must help those within our sphere of influence to be faithful to God so that they may enjoy the blessing of eternity around God's throne. We need each other; we really do. I hope this lesson will help us to accept, consider and be devoted to one another with the love of Christ Jesus, our Lord.

CHAPTER 11

Be at Peace with One Another

"Salt is good, but if it loses its saltiness, how can you make it salty again? Have salt in yourselves, and be at peace with each other."
(Mark 9:50)

In the greatest sermon ever preached (the Sermon on the Mount), Jesus Christ began with what has come to be called "The Beatitudes." They consist of eight statements about what will make one "blessed" or truly happy as he seeks to serve and obey God. The one I want to focus on in this chapter is found in Matthew 5:9. "Blessed are the peacemakers, for they will be called the sons of God." Notice that the Lord did not say, "Blessed are the peace lovers" or "Blessed are the peace talkers" or "Blessed are the peace dreamers," but rather, "Blessed are the peacemakers." It is, therefore, the duty of every child of God to do all he can to work for peace and unity in the church.

God's Desire

Clearly, God desires that his people live and serve together in an atmosphere of love, peace and harmony. He is displeased when there is division, strife and contention.

The first century church at Corinth is an example of a divided church and the apostle Paul's inspired teaching was intended to correct the sinful conditions within the congregation. "I appeal to you, brothers, in the name of our Lord Jesus Christ, that all of you agree with one another so that there may be no divisions among you and that you may be perfectly united in mind and thought" (1 Corinthians 1:10). Some were committed to following after one teacher and some after others. "My brothers, some from Chloe's household have informed me that there are quarrels among you. What I mean is this: One of you says, 'I follow Paul'; another, 'I follow Apollos'; another, 'I follow Cephas'; still another, 'I follow Christ.' Is Christ divided? Was Paul crucified for you? Were you baptized into the name of Paul? I am thankful that I did not baptize any of you except Crispus and Gaius, so no one can say that you were baptized into my name. (Yes, I also baptized the household of Stephanas; beyond that, I don't remember if I baptized anyone else)" (verses 13-16). Such splintering and division is an abomination to God. There is no indication that the teachers themselves were to be blamed for this situation. If they did contribute to it, they were to be blamed also.

Paul told them, in no uncertain terms, that they needed to grow up spiritually and get along with each other. "Brothers, I could not address you as spiritual but as worldly—mere infants in Christ. I gave you milk, not solid food, for you were not yet ready for it. Indeed, you are still not ready. You are still worldly. For since there is jealousy and quarreling among you, are you not worldly? Are you not acting like mere men? For when one says, 'I follow Paul,' and another, 'I follow Apollos,' are you not mere men?" (1 Corinthians 3:1-4). There should be no place among the people of God for envy, strife, jealousies, quarreling and division. He then reminds them that these Bible teachers they so admired were all on the same team and were co-workers with God. "What, after all, is Apollos? And what is Paul? Only servants, through whom you came to believe—as the Lord assigned to each his task. I planted the seed, Apollos watered it, but God made it grow. So neither he who plants nor he who waters is anything, but only God, who makes things grow. The man who plants and the man who waters have one purpose, and each one will be rewarded according to his own labor. For we are God's fellow workers; you are God's field, God's building" (verses 5-9). The totally unselfish attitude shown here by Paul should be our attitude as well. Work together in peace; give God all the glory; hide yourself behind the cross of Christ and watch the Lord give the increase.

Do you remember the prayer of Christ in John 17? He said, in verse 11, about the original apostles: "I will remain in the world no longer, but they are still in the world, and I am coming to you. Holy Father, protect them by the power of your name—the name you gave me—so that they may be one as we are one." Then he went on, in verses 20-23, to include us today: "My prayer is not for them (the apostles) alone. I pray also for those who will believe in me through their message, that all of them may be one, Father, just as you are in me and I am in you. May they also be in us so that the world may believe that you have sent me. I have given them the glory that you gave me, that they may be one as we are one: I in them and you in me. May they be brought to complete unity to let the world know that you sent me and have loved them even as you have loved me." Jesus prayed, not for something that was impossible, but for the reality that the people of God would be one, as he and the Father are one. That was the prayer of our Savior for his body. That was his desire for his church, the church for which he died.

One other passage that ought to convince us, if we still need to be convinced, that God wants that kind of harmonious relationships in the church is 1 Thessalonians 5:12-13. "Now we ask you, brothers, to respect those who work hard among you, who are over you in the Lord and who admonish you. Hold them in the highest regard in love because of their work. Live in peace with each other." One of the best things a local church can do for its leadership is simply to be at peace, to work out any problems among themselves so that they don't grow and develop into a church-wide problem.

The word "peace" is found eighty-eight times in the New Testament and is contained in every book of the New Testament. God is referred to as the "God of peace" five times in the New Testament (Romans 15:33; Romans 16:20; Philippians 4:9; 1 Thessalonians 5:23; Hebrews 13:20). Notice this sample verse. "The God of peace will soon crush Satan under your feet. The grace of our Lord Jesus be with you" (Romans 16:20).

Jesus was prophesied as coming into the world to be the "Prince of Peace" (Isaiah 9:6). This idea of peace and harmony is obviously very important to God.

Not Always Easy

Although such peace is clearly the will of God, this kind of unity and harmony is not achieved easily. There are barriers to that. There are difficulties that Satan places in our way in an attempt to disrupt the harmony and unity that should exist in a local church.

In Romans 12:18, for instance, Paul pointed out the reality of this difficulty. "If it is possible, as far as it depends on you, live at peace with everyone." After beginning the statement with the word "if," he then says that only part of it depends on you. The other part, of course, belongs to the other person. It takes at least two people to live in peace and harmony with each other. And so he tells us that you must make certain, that if there is disunity, it is the other guy's problem and not yours. Peace, therefore, will not always be possible. For those who are unwilling to accept truth, with them there cannot be peace. We cannot compromise the truth of the gospel in order to get along with other people. Within the confines of the word of God is where peace and harmony must be found and maintained. With people who are unwilling to accept, practice, teach and live by the word of God, there cannot be that kind of peace. But the point is to be sure that such division is not your fault.

In Ephesians 4:1-3, Paul had this to say. "As a prisoner for the Lord, then, I urge you to live a life worthy of the calling you have received. Be completely humble and gentle; be patient, bearing with one another in love. Make every effort to keep the unity of the Spirit through the bond of peace." Verse 3 is one of my favorite verses. As Christians, we all have an obligation, as peacemakers for God, to make every effort to keep the unity of the Spirit in the bond of peace. That's what God wants. That's our responsibility as the people of God—to maintain that kind of unity and peace. But notice that this is going to take some effort on our part. The New King James uses the word "endeavoring" toward peace. It's a job that you undertake. If you endeavor to cut down a dead tree in your yard or to wash and wax your car, you are going to have to put some work into it. That's what an endeavor is. Results don't happen easily or accidentally. And what that indicates to us, once again, is the responsibility of every Christian, not just a select few to do this. Every child of God, who claims to be a disciple of Jesus Christ, must contribute to that kind of peace.

We do so, first of all, by making certain that we have the right attitude. We must not be quarreling and arguing and being difficult to get along with. We do so, secondly, by helping others who may have some differences, and therefore, some degree of conflict, to get along. We become peacemakers first in our minds as we determine that, if there is a problem, I will not be the source of it. And secondly, if others are causing conflict, and I can do something to help that situation, that's exactly what I must do.

Things Which Make for Peace

Notice what Paul taught in Romans 14:19. "Let us therefore make every effort to do what leads to peace and to mutual edification." He encourages us to actively look for and pursue (follow after, KJV) things that will contribute to peace and harmony. What kinds of things, then, will bring peace in a local church? What attitudes should we have? What kinds of actions should characterize our lives so that we have the unity and peace that God desires?

Let's go back to Ephesians 4 and notice that Paul wrote, in verse one, that as followers of Christ, he wants us to have a walk worthy of our calling. He then continues in verse 2 and actually defines that for us—"Be completely humble and gentle; be patient, bearing with one another in love." He uses four phrases to tell us how we can keep the unity of the Spirit. Let's examine each of these for a moment.

1. **Be completely humble.**

   The first thing that is going to contribute to peace is humility (all lowliness, NKJV). The opposite of that, of course, would be arrogance, conceit, selfishness or elevating oneself above others. Rather, we must have humility in our hearts. Have you ever known someone who was always right about everything? You've probably worked with someone like that or gone to school with him over the years—someone who knew everything about everything and was never wrong. It's hard to be at peace with someone like that because, occasionally, everyone is wrong about something. And if a person feels he is never wrong about anything, there is going to be conflict.

2. **Be completely gentle.**

   We all know what is means to be gentle with others. All you have to do to witness gentleness is to watch a mother holding a newborn baby— carefully, gently, lovingly. The opposite of being gentle would be being harsh or rude. Some people attempt to justify rudeness in their way of life and in their speech by saying, "People always know where I stand about things. I speak my mind. I let people know what I think." But sometimes, we just need to keep what we think to ourselves. The Bible says that, "A fool vents all his feelings, but a wise man keeps them to himself" (Proverbs 29:11, NKJV). There are times and circumstances when our response would be harsh, and, therefore, we do not respond, at least, not quickly, because we would not respond gently, as the circumstance would require. If we can tell the difference between someone who is harsh and someone who is gentle and recognize that harshness and rudeness contribute to disunity, that gentleness with each other (even in times when we need to be firm) leads to peace, then we can understand the need to be gentle.

3. Be patient.

The next quality Paul describes is to be patient (longsuffering, NKJV) with others. Patience means that we are willing to endure or persevere through a circumstance. One who is impatient wants something right now and is unwilling to wait, unwilling for any time to pass before what he wants comes true. We need to be characterized by patience and endurance because change does not happen overnight. When you talk to people about changes they need to make in their lives, they may not immediately agree. They may need time to think about what you have said. They may need to be given time to repent of sin. It's hard for most people to admit that there may be changes they need to make. And so we must be patient with each other. There comes a time even when God's patience runs out, as in the days of Noah. It was 120 years before God finally brought the flood of destruction upon the ungodly. But his patience eventually ran out and he destroyed the world. We are not saying we must forever put up with sin in people's lives, but rather that we must give them time to do the right thing so that peace and harmony can exist.

4. Bear with one another in love.

The fourth thing Paul mentions that makes for peace and that we must endeavor to put into our lives is forbearance, bearing with one another in love. That means being willing to tolerate some differences in personalities, backgrounds, and circumstances that have brought people to the point of conflict. We are not talking about accepting and ignoring sin in other's lives. But, because we love each other, we are willing to tolerate some differences. In a church where I preached in Illinois, there was a sister who was always cold, no matter what the temperature was outside. Her husband controlled the thermostat, so guess what the rest of us did. We got hot at services (maybe in more ways than one). But most people took it good-naturedly and were willing to put up with that because she and, no doubt, others were so cold-natured that they were extremely uncomfortable unless the temperature in the building was way up there. We are all "wired" differently about various things. We must accept some of those differences to accept others.

While we are in Ephesians 4 and looking at things that contribute to peace, notice verse 32. "Be kind and compassionate to one another, forgiving each other, just as in Christ God forgave you." Here are three more qualities of those who would be peacemakers

1. Kind

2. Compassionate

3. Forgiving of others

Because there are going to be differences in personality in any local church, when you get enough people together, conflict is inevitable. It is going to happen. We must realize that we need to deal with those differences in a loving and kind way, being compassionate (tenderhearted, NKJV) toward the needs, feelings and emotions of others and when real transgressions have occurred, rather than holding a grudge and being bitter toward each other, we must forgive one another. And he reminds us that God has already forgiven us, even when we didn't deserve to be forgiven.

In all of these things we have talked about, being humble, being gentle, being patient, bearing with one another in love, being kind and compassionate, and forgiving others, I want you to realize that all of them are qualities of the heart. They are things on the inside of us. They are not really things we do, as much as what we are, on the inside. They are attitudes we have toward other people that will determine whether conflict exists and is dealt with in a proper way or whether, because of those conflicts, disunity and disharmony exist.

Things That Destroy Peace

Let's think, for a little while, about the other side of the coin. If there are qualities of the heart that lead to peace, then what are some things that lead to division? What will destroy peace in a local church?

Bitterness, anger and slander

Since we are still in Ephesians 4, let's look at verse 31. "Get rid of all bitterness, rage and anger, brawling and slander, along with every form of malice." What an ugly list of undesirable qualities. Bitterness between brothers and sisters in Christ will not in any way contribute to peace, nor will rage and anger, brawling and slander. The slander he speaks of here is translated as "evil speaking" in other versions of the New Testament. It refers to speaking evil about one another, saying terrible things to each other and to the world about those who are part of the family of God. Malice involves wanting bad things to happen to others, wishing the worst for them, rather than the best. Can you imagine Christians feeling that way about their fellow disciples? What he is telling us, in case we don't realize it, is that these things lead away from peace and harmony. The people of God need to get rid of all these sinful attitudes and actions. Let these things be put far away from our minds and hearts.

Assume for just a moment, that you and I have a problem about something. Is it going to help the situation for me to go around and slander you before other people? Is it going to make for a stronger church for me to tell others about all the supposedly bad things you've said and done? Is it going to help if I grow bitter and hold a grudge against you? No, none of those things will lead to peace and none of those reactions will, therefore, please God.

It might, somehow, make me feel better on the inside to talk about you (probably not, in reality), but it's definitely not going to help the church. Rather, it can only harm and damage the cause of Christ. People will not be stronger in their faith because of such actions. No one will be edified by that kind of behavior. The only way that situation can be resolved is either for you and me to get together and work out our differences or for a third party (a peacemaker) to get us together and help us resolve the conflict. But bitterness, wrath, anger and slander ought to be put away.

The anger he speaks about here is being quick-tempered. It is not righteous indignation at sin. Jesus got angry about sin in people's lives. He rebuked them at times about sin. He always did so in love and to bring them into harmony with the will of God. But being quick-tempered in our dealings with one another is not helpful and it's not biblical. It's just not right.

Selfishness and gossip

It's also not right to be selfish, always having to have things my way. People rarely say it, but often, their attitude is "my way or no way." If you don't do things exactly as I want, we're going to have a problem. In Galatians 5:15, Paul speaks of "biting and devouring each other" until we are "destroyed by each other." It's important for us not to bite and consume one another in the things we say and do. In James 1:19-20, James said, by inspiration, "My dear brothers, take note of this: Everyone should be quick to listen, slow to speak and slow to become angry, for man's anger does not bring about the righteous life that God desires." Too often, we are swift to speak but slow to listen to the other guy's side of the story. We need to remember that, in almost every situation, there are two sides to every story, two sides to every conflict, one that is right and one that is wrong. We must listen to the other person's view and perspective, being eager to listen and slow to respond. Even in a circumstance where anger may be appropriate, we must be slow to get angry with our brothers and sisters in the Lord. We must be cautious, again, about the problem of gossip or slander, talking about others and/or listening about others. Gossip is both a sin of the tongue and a sin of the ear. If we refuse to listen to gossip, it will die. But when we provide a ready and willing audience, to listen to anything that someone wants to say about anyone else, then we must realize that we are just as guilty of gossip as those who are doing the speaking. The Bible speaks of those who have "itching ears." They just can't wait to hear the latest "dirt" on someone else and especially if it's a Christian they've had a problem with in the past.

An argumentative spirit

As well, we must guard against possessing an argumentative spirit. Some people always want to argue about everything. (Some will even argue that they don't like to argue!) Notice 2 Timothy 2:23. "Don't have anything to do with foolish and stupid arguments, because you know they produce quarrels." There are some foolish things that have divided churches. These things should never have been a problem between two Christians, let alone two groups of Christians who have now decided that they just can't worship together. Paul tells us to avoid that kind of dispute, knowing it generates strife. They destroy peace. He goes on, in verses 24-26 and says, "And the Lord's servant must not quarrel; instead, he must be kind to everyone, able to teach, not resentful. Those who oppose him he must gently instruct, in the hope that God will grant them repentance leading them to a knowledge of the truth, and that they will come to their senses and escape from the trap of the devil, who has taken them captive to do his will." Do you see, again, that he says we should handle such problems with gentleness and humility, not going on the attack, not trying to out-shout, out-argue, or out-quarrel others, but patiently correcting those who are in opposition, that they may come to their senses spiritually.

A desire for power

In 3 John 9-10, we are introduced to a man named Diotrephes, who was causing division among the people of God by his desire for pre-eminence. "I wrote to the church, but Diotrephes, who loves to be first, will have nothing to do with us. So if I come, I will call attention to what he is doing, gossiping maliciously about us. Not satisfied with that, he refuses to welcome the brothers. He also stops those who want to do so and puts them out of the church." Diotrephes wanted to be the boss. He imposed his will on everyone else. The next verse warns us not to follow such an evil spirit. "Dear friend, do not imitate what is evil but what is good" (verse 11). It is not easy to stand up to one whose desire for power leads to such abuses.

But it is important for the sake of the ultimate peace of the congregation to oppose those who would behave so. Don't be like Diotrephes.

Conclusion

If I could convince us of one thing, all of these problems would disappear. We must always remember that the enemy is the devil, not each other. We are on the same team. We all want to go to the same place—heaven. And we need to help each other get there as well. We must see each other in that light, not as enemies, but as helpers, as friends, as brothers and sisters in Christ. Even when we disagree with someone, we can work out those differences in love.

I grew up with two younger sisters and it's amazing how much we disagreed, argued and fought during those early years. But, in spite of those differences, we never stopped loving each other. That's the way it is in the church. We are family, brothers and sisters in the Lord, and we will be that even in times of disagreement. The devil is our enemy and he wants to take as many of us as possible to hell with him. It's our duty to help each other make it to heaven.

There are two benefits to be enjoyed from being a people at peace with God and one another. First, it leads to a blessed life here. The beatitude of Jesus says that those who are peacemakers will be called "the sons of God." Philippians 4:7 promises us that "the peace of God, which transcends all understanding, will guard your hearts and your minds in Christ Jesus." Secondly, and most importantly, it leads to eternal life in heaven. "Make every effort to live in peace with all men and to be holy; without holiness no one will see the Lord" (Hebrews 12:14). God will eternally reward those who seek peace and holiness.

Are you fulfilling your part of this "one another" responsibility?

CHAPTER 12

Love One Another

"Dear friends, since God so loved us, we also ought to love one
another. No one has ever seen God; but if we love one another,
God lives in us and his love is made complete in us."
(1 John 4:11-12)

There is a legend about the apostle John and his last days on the earth.
It is said that after he was returned from his exile on Patmos, he
went to Ephesus where he lived and served the church until his death.
Whenever he was asked to speak, he would stand before the assembly and
say, "Little children, love one another" and then he would sit down. That's
it; that was his entire sermon. "Little children, love one another."

Of course, we have no way of knowing if that story is true or not. But we
know it is true that John was present, along with the other apostles, when
Jesus told them, in John 13:34-35, "A new command I give you: Love one
another. As I have loved you, so you must love one another. By this all men
will know that you are my disciples, if you love one another."

Remember all of those "one another" commands we have been studying?
Believers are taught to be at peace with one another, be devoted to, give
preference to, be like-minded with, receive, encourage, greet, care for,
serve, bear one another's burdens, be kind to, forgive, submit to, bear
with, teach, comfort, exhort, consider, confess to, have compassion for,
be hospitable to, and to love one another. Would it surprise you to know

that the most often repeated of all of those responsibilities is to love one another?

Let's consider three important things about our love for each other.

1. This is how the world will know we are true disciples.

"By this all men will know that you are my disciples, if you love one another" (John 13:35). This is the divinely given mark of discipleship. This is how we can prove to the world that we are truly the Lord's.

What is the church where you attend generally known for? If you have any reputation in town, what do people think of when they hear of that congregation? Largest church in town? A well-known preacher? Newest building in the best part of the city? Shouldn't we do our best to be known as the people who really love one another? Be honest. Would love for each other be an identifying mark of your own church home?

Jesus repeatedly said to his disciples that they were to love each other. See John 15:12, 17 and many others. I get the impression that this is important to the Savior. And remember that the apostles were not soft, sissy types. They were hardened fishermen, a relentless tax collector, a religious zealot. Not exactly "wear your emotions on your sleeve" kind of guys. When the Lord told them to love each other, that was just something that people who mutually shared a loving Master would do.

There may well be other obstacles to converting the world, especially in our day and time. But we need to do a better job of being as loving, caring, serving followers of the Lord.

2. Without love, nothing else matters.

"If I speak in the tongues of men and of angels, but have not love, I am only a resounding gong or a clanging cymbal. If I have the gift of prophecy and can fathom all mysteries and all knowledge, and if I have a faith that can move mountains, but have not love, I am nothing. If I give all I possess to the poor and surrender my body to the flames, but have not love, I gain nothing" (1 Corinthians 13:1-3).

Our motives and attitudes are important to God. *Why* we do things ranks right up there with *what* we actually do in the Lord's eyes.

So that no one would misunderstand what he was talking about, Paul went on to explain what love is and what love does. "Love is patient, love is kind. It does not envy, it does not boast, it is not proud. It is not rude, it is not self-seeking, it is not easily angered, it keeps no record of wrongs. Love does not delight in evil but rejoices with the truth. It always protects, always trusts, always hopes, always perseveres. Love never fails (verses 4-8a).

Several years ago, I paraphrased 1 Corinthians 13:1-3 to reflect some important truths we need to understand. "Although I talk about love, if I am not showing it by kindness, it means nothing. Even if I attend all of the services, sing with all my heart and observe the Lord's Supper faithfully, if I don't have love, I am in real spiritual trouble. And if I preach lots of sermons, teach Bible classes, grade Bible correspondence courses, am appointed as an elder or a deacon, but don't really love my brothers and sisters, I won't go to heaven."

3. Love requires actions, not just words.

"Dear children, let us not love with words or tongue but with actions and in truth" (1 John 3:18).

It is pretty easy to say "I love you" to someone. But are you really there for them when things get tough and they need you the most? It is even easy to talk about loving others in Bible classes, but then what do we do about it?

It was storming one night and the little boy was awakened by a loud clap of thunder. He saw the lightning flashing outside and called out to his parents, "Would someone come in here and sleep with me?" His sleepy parents responded, "No, you'll be fine; Just go back to sleep and remember that God loves you." After a brief pause, the little boy said, "Yeah, I know, but I want love with skin on it." I think that's how we all feel. We want love with skin on it.

In context, notice verses 16 and 17. "This is how we know what love is: Jesus Christ laid down his life for us. And we ought to lay down our lives for our brothers. If anyone has material possessions and sees his brother in need but has no pity on him, how can the love of God be in him?" These verses are not saying that Jesus died for mankind, they are showing us that He lived for mankind. And that's how we are to show our love for one another, in the things we do for others. It's not a matter of how good a game we talk, but how are we doing? What are we doing? And why are we doing those things? This makes all the difference in the world. John tells us that the love of God is not in one who will not show his love for others in visible ways, with concrete deeds of service. Even if we proclaim loudly to the world about how much we love God, the world can see and God knows better.

Augustine said:

> "What does love look like? It has hands to help others. It has feet to hasten to the poor and needy. It has eyes to see misery and want. It has ears to hear the sighs and sorrows of men. That is what love looks like."

Romans 12:9-10 tells us "Love must be sincere. Hate what is evil; cling to what is good. Be devoted to one another in brotherly love. Honor one another above yourselves." The idea in these verses is that love must be without hypocrisy, that is, we must make it real, not an external show to impress others. It is important that our love for each other be genuine, not merely something we force ourselves to accomplish in some legalistic way.

The context gives us some examples of practical ways we can show our love for others (verses 11ff). "Share with God's people who are in need. Practice hospitality" (verse 13). "Rejoice with those who rejoice; mourn with those who mourn" (verse 15). "Live in harmony with one another. Do not be proud, but be willing to associate with people of low position. Do not be conceited" (verse 16).

Let's look at three more passages on this subject of loving one another.

- 1 Peter 1:22—"Now that you have purified yourselves by obeying the truth so that you have sincere love for your brothers, love one another deeply, from the heart."

Peter insists here again that our love must be "sincere." The King James Version uses the word "unfeigned," which comes from a Greek word that literally means unhypocrisy. Of course, we have no such word in English, but we can clearly see the meaning in that idea. There can be no room for hypocrisy in the love we have for one another. He is telling us, don't just pretend to love others. Don't be one thing to another's face and something else behind his back. We would not want to be treated that way and must not so treat others.

Peter also emphasizes that we are to love "with a pure heart"—from the very depths of our being. This is not to be shallow or meaningless, but heartfelt, from the soul.

He further instructs us that this love is to be felt "deeply." "Fervently" is the way the New King James renders that word and it denotes something that is strained, stretched, with determination, seriously, earnestly.

- 1 Peter 3:8—"Finally, all of you, live in harmony with one another; be sympathetic, love as brothers, be compassionate and humble."

He first tells disciples in that passage to live in peace and harmony. He then reminds us to "love as brothers," which refers to the family love we are to have for one another. One of the greatest blessings God has given us is the family we enjoy through our relationships in the church. The church, when it functions as God designed it, is a taste of heaven on earth. When we fall short of being what God wants us to be, it can give people a distorted view of our eternal reward.

Notice that the thought continues into verse 9. "Do not repay evil with evil or insult with insult, but with blessing, because to this you were called so that you may inherit a blessing." In other words, there will be times when we hurt, mistreat or misunderstand each other. How are we to react then? What does love require of us?

If you are mistreated by others, what does he tell you to do? Return a blessing. Don't try to get even; don't try to punish them; don't try to hurt them more than they have hurt you. Repay evil with good.

- 1 John 4:7-12—"Dear friends, let us love one another, for love comes from God. Everyone who loves has been born of God and knows

God. Whoever does not love does not know God, because God is love. This is how God showed his love among us: He sent his one and only Son into the world that we might live through him. This is love: not that we loved God, but that he loved us and sent his Son as an atoning sacrifice for our sins. Dear friends, since God so loved us, we also ought to love one another. No one has ever seen God; but if we love one another, God lives in us and his love is made complete in us."

How much we love shows how well we know God. We cannot claim to love and serve God if we are not showing our love toward our fellow Christians. The more we love, the more we are like God. Therefore, if we are not loving, as we ought to be, we are not like God. We are never more like him than when we love others.

Conclusion

Remember that love is a two-way street. Don't be just a "user." Be a giver. Even when others don't act like they should, continue to love them. Don't forget that God loved us while we were still sinners (Romans 5:8) and sent His Son to die in our place.

One final thought. The apostle Peter wrote these words in 1 Peter 4:8: "Above all, love one another deeply, because love covers a multitude of sins." The New King James renders that first phrase as, "Above all things, have fervent love for one another." I find it amazing, in some ways, that Peter says that our love for each other is important above all things. There are many important lessons in 1st and 2nd Peter. Over and above all of them, Peter tells us to love one another. And he says that love "will cover a multitude of sins." We are all going to make mistakes, just as a husband and wife do in their relationship with each other. But we are to give one another the benefit of the doubt and not allow those mistakes and problems to come between us.

My prayer for you is the same as that of Paul for the first century Thessalonians. "Now about brotherly love we do not need to write to you, for you yourselves have been taught by God to love each other. And in fact, you do love all the brothers throughout Macedonia. Yet we urge you, brothers, to do so more and more" (1 Thessalonians 4:9-10). May our love for one another abound more and more as time goes on.

"Little children, love one another."

25033123R00070

Made in the USA
Columbia, SC
01 September 2018